MW00989368

UNVEILED HOPE

SCOTTY SMITH
AND
MICHAEL CARD

A JANET THOMA BOOK

THOMAS NELSON PUBLISHERS
Nashville • Atlanta • London • Vancouver
Printed in the United States of America

Copyright © 1997 by Scotty Smith and Michael Card

All rights reserved. Written permission must be secured from the publisher to use or reproduce any part of this book, except for brief quotations in critical reviews or articles.

Published in Nashville, Tennessee, by Thomas Nelson, Inc., Publishers, and distributed in Canada by Word Communications, Ltd., Richmond, British Columbia.

The Bible version used in this publication is the HOLY BIBLE, NEW INTERNATIONAL VERSION®. Copyright © 1973, 1978, 1984 by International Bible Society. Used by permission of Zondervan Publishing House. All rights reserved.

Scripture quotations noted KJV are from THE KING JAMES VERSION of the Holy Bible.

Library of Congress Cataloging-in-Publication Data

Smith, Scotty, 1950–
    Unveiled hope : eternal encouragement from the book of
Revelation / Scotty Smith and Michael Card.
        p.   cm.
    Includes bibliographical references.
    ISBN 0-7852-7209-7
    1. Bible. N.T. Revelation—Criticism, interpretation, etc.
I. Card, Michael, 1957—   . II. Title.
BL2825.2.S654 1997
228'.06—dc21   96–52485
                                                     CIP

Printed in the United States of America.

2 3 4 5 6 BVG 02 01 00 99 98 97

To our incredible wives, Darlene Smith and Susan Card, with whom we groan inwardly and wait expectantly for the unveiling of the new heavens and the new earth. We are rich men indeed, to be so well loved by you.

And in loving memory of Dr. Jack Miller who taught us to say and believe . . . "Cheer up! You're a lot worse off than you think. Cheer up! But you're a lot more accepted and loved than you ever dreamed possible, because the gospel is true."

Jack, thanks for teaching us and showing us that heaven has already begun because of the "gospel of God's grace."

CONTENTS

ACKNOWLEDGMENTS

Where do I begin and where do I end in mentioning and thanking those who have been a part of helping me through the conception, labor, and delivery of this book? Here are a few of God's gifts of grace to me:

To Darlene, Kristin, and Scott: Thanks for being my loving and encouraging family. I love you more than I know how to express.

To my dad and brother, Moose: Each year I am more aware of God's gift of you to me.

To Steve Crotts: Thanks for dragging me to the Billy Graham movie, *The Restless Ones*, in March 1968. It was there I surrendered to the mercy, grace, and love of Jesus.

To J. L. and Patt Williams: Thanks for discipling me in those first years in the faith. You gave me a love for the Word and the work of Jesus among the nations.

To Rose Marie Miller: Thanks for being my mom in faith, my hero, prayer partner, and friend. You simply amaze me.

To Scott Roley: Thanks for being more than a best friend. You have invited me to honesty, vulnerability, passion, joy, and a deep thirst to drink in God's grace and the fullness of life, which of course includes fly fishing.

To Marvin and Phoebe Nischan: Thanks for showing me the servant heart of Jesus all the years I've had the joy of knowing you. And a big thanks for first taking me to Switzerland. You are priceless friends.

To Ron and Priscilla Davis: Thanks for extending the

welcoming heart of God to me when this book was conceived at Chalet Edelweiss; the last year she was yours.

To Anita and Walter Oglive, thanks for being new friends and conduits of God's grace for Darlene and me at Peacock Hill Country Inn—one more little taste of the final rest and joy that awaits us.

To my circle of friends in "Rapture and Rupture": Bill and Nancy Puryear, Buddy Greene, Clyde Godwin, Bruce and Debbie McCurdy, Wayne and Pat Dunn, Bob Briner, Wes and Fran King, Malcolm Greenwood, Sue Smith, Laura Pollock, Bob and Marion Allen, Steven Curtis and Mary Beth Chapman, Charlie and Andi Ashworth, Penny Nelms, Steve and Mary Jean Green, Wes and Stephanie Coker, Charlie and Zonie Compton, Geoff and Jan Moore, and a host of other prayer warriors and encouragers.

To the congregation of Christ Community Church: Thanks for ten years of groaning and growing with me in grace!

To Janet Thoma and the whole support family at Thomas Nelson: Thanks for pushing me and giving me encouragement when I needed it the most. I am so glad this first one is done!

—Scotty Smith

LETTERS TO OUR READERS

A Letter from Scotty Smith

Mike Card and I have been walking together as brothers and friends since 1980. This project is born out of that treasured relationship, one which is marked by a shared calling and commitment to help the people of God understand the Word of God.

I am a rich man, indeed, to have someone like Mike who "loves at all times." We have been through many seasons of life together in our growing as men, husbands, dads, servants of God, and stewards of His grace. He is one of a handful of friends who encouraged me to plant a church in Franklin, Tennessee, ten years ago, despite my fears and reluctance. He still encourages me as his pastor.

We know each other's strengths and weaknesses, dreams and heartaches, passions and joys. When the phone rings and Mike is on the other end, he will ask me, "How ya doin'?" Those three words convey a whole lot more than an invitation to chat. He wants to know about my heart, even as I want to know of his. We are committed to "provoke one another to love and good deeds," and to "bear one another's burden." For years he has trusted me to go over the freshly written lyrics of his songs to make sure that they are biblically and theologically accurate.

No one in Christian music is more committed to creatively and faithfully presenting the truths of Scripture. Only a small percentage of those who have listened to Mike's music through the years realize, however, that he would rather lead a small Bible study group than sing to a full auditorium. In his eyes his talents as a musician are the equivalent of the apostle Paul's "tent making." By using them he is able to be about his greatest passion: teaching the Bible. How I thank God for Mike's "tent making" and his skill as a teacher. Both bring the Word to life.

It is, therefore, both a great joy and an honor to be involved in this book and recording project with Mike. I have to admit that I feel every bit the rookie in this equation, a little like a batboy helping Babe Ruth or a first-year Suzuki violin student assisting Stradivarius! But my friend has been quite encouraging as I am learning to make the difficult transition from communicating with a microphone in my hand to the medium of the printed page. Thank God our relationship is full of His grace!

It is our prayer that this tapestry of our lives, stories, and labors will bring much glory to God and deep encouragement to the followers of the Lamb. We long to see the hope of the gospel, so profoundly expressed in Revelation, made real to other hungry and thirsty hearts.

A Letter from Michael Card

I have spent much time in the company of John and his gospel, and yet it has always been hard for me to grasp the notion that the same man who wrote about Jesus' life with such simple elegance could have also written the riot that is Revelation. How could the same dear soul who spoke with such compassion about the just and gentle Jesus also write with such ferocity about the avenging One with the sword in His mouth?

If you look through your NIV Bible you will see small poetic fragments set aside in the text of Revelation. These are believed to be either fragments of ancient hymns (see also Phil. 2:6–11) used by the early church or else brief songs and poems John heard during his visionary experience. These fragments provided the body of lyrical content for both my short essays as well as the accompanying album. As I struggled to put these fragments to music, the text of Revelation itself began to sing; the pieces started falling into place.

Through this process I have come to almost feel sorry for people who have not been made to go through the same ordeal of trying to put this text to music. Since I was not able to hear the lyrics in their original musical setting—for indeed that ancient setting has been lost—I was to forced to listen to them in my own way.

Rarely did I hear these fragments in the "Handelesque" setting, in which we are all used to imagining the music of heaven. Instead I heard joyful Irish reels and the powerful strains of Black gospel choirs. Some settings seemed best put into acoustic style, others in a more driving rock. In short, I heard Revelation in the music of my own time.

As I listened to the music of the text, I realized that is precisely what John requires of all his readers. John provides the words, we provide the music of our imaginations to make the text come alive by the Spirit.

You might be tempted to conclude, "Sure, he's a musician. He thinks in music." And to a certain extent you may be correct. Yet I have come to believe that even as Revelation is supposed to be experienced with the eyes of the imagination (One of my professors told me once that when you read of the horsemen of the apocalypse you should be prepared to leap out of the way!), so also it is designed to be listened to with the ears of the imagination. And that means not lazily relying on professional musicians, but listening to the music of the apocalypse on our own.

This book and the album are the fruit of friendship, shared gifts, pain, fun, and a longing for the return of our blessed God and Savior, Jesus Christ. The format is somewhat unique. First, Scotty's essays into the thematic exposition of the book of Revelation, and then the lyrics of my songs (from the companion album "Unveiled Hope") and my essays. When you listen to the music on the album, you will hear the sounds and remember the message.

This collaboration is one of the first from our little community, and I hope it will not be the last. It was born out of many walks and much conversation over meal fellowship. Scotty's approach delivered me from the artificial attempt to unravel the mystery of Revelation. Instead he helped me to see that the One being revealed in the Revelation is the very Person we all desire most to see: Jesus Christ Himself.

Perhaps the initial reason for my difficulty in grasping John's Revelation was not the seeming disparity between the Apocalypse and his gospel, but the seeming disparity between the Jesus revealed in each work. In the gospel, Jesus is on the whole so gentle. In the Apocalypse, He roars. But this difference is as false and artificial as the distinction many make between the God of the Old Testament and the God of the New.

John wants us to understand that they both are the same Jesus. The heartbreaking beauty of His second coming is no less aweight with His glory than His first coming. The Word made flesh, who walked dusty roads to share the good news of the coming kingdom, is the same as the Rider on the war horse aflame with holiness.

Introduction

The Fulfillment of Our Great Hope

As I write these words I am sitting at the foot of the Swiss Alps in the little fishing village of Iseltwald, just outside of Interlaken. Never have I seen bluer skies—with a richness of hue that betrays description. I can feel the fiery warmth of the fall colors in the trees along the ridge of the Alps. And I can taste the pure vanilla of the fresh white morning snow. Is there something that can be called too beautiful?

Before me is Lake Brienz whose blue-green waters seem so vast, so inviting, so absolutely calming. No tempest, just a tapestry of peacefulness that resonates with something deep in the core of my soul.

It is so good to be here, right now, drinking in this astonishing vision—for it has been a hard year, really, a hard season of life. So many changes, so many demands. I don't know when spiritual warfare has seemed as intense. Good friends are overwhelmed. Family members are facing loss and the adjustments forced by advancing years. Maybe that's why this setting is just drawing me in.

The quiet of this place is so pronounced. All I can hear is the rolling movement of a passenger train on the other side of the lake, making its way to the wood-carving village of Brienz. The aroma of baking bread is wafting up from the kitchen below as I sit on my balcony. I watch as an older Swiss gentleman rhythmically hand sickles grass on the steep hillside just below me. To my left, a family of cows graze, with brown eyes as big as bagels. I want to run, to laugh, to sing, to share this scene with those I love. But I am reluctant to disrupt this precious, holy moment. Surely, I was made for this.

"Lord, can I stay here? What a gift this day is! Your timing could not be better. I've got an idea! I'll set up three shelters or at least a three-bedroom chalet for you and Moses and Elijah, right here, right now!"

This may seem more like a Swiss travelogue than an introduction to a book about Revelation. Yet as I sit here I cannot think of a more appropriate setting for me to begin my writing, a context which gives expression to the two driving forces that are compelling me to hammer out my heart on this laptop computer: The first is a near obsession to get the book of Revelation and its liberating visions back into the hands and hearts of God's sons and daughters. The second is a longing to see my family, my friends, the congregation I am so privileged to pastor, and God's people in general, filled with the living hope that Jesus has won for us. These twin voices encouraged this entire work. Let me briefly speak to each.

A Longing to Get Revelation Back Into the Hands of the People

Many friends have said to me, "Scotty, why in the world would you tackle Revelation as the focus of your very first book? Are you crazy? Or just presumptuous?"

No, but I am somewhat angry. That anger is similar to the apostle Paul's emotion after he had faithfully preached salvation by grace through faith. Certain men came down from Jerusalem and started distorting the gospel by insisting that the male Gentile converts had to be circumcised in order to be fully recognized as Christians. In effect, these legalists were preaching "another gospel which is no gospel at all."

They were putting the Galatian converts back under the very law from which Jesus had set them free. Paul went pastorally and theologically ballistic! He knew, as Martin Luther would say later on the eve of the Reformation, "Bad theology is the worst taskmaster of all." The entire book of Galatians is written to undo the damage of those Jerusalem legalists.

In a similar way I am stirred up at how the book of Revelation has suffered at the hands of its many interpreters though the years, and especially those of recent generations. Many simply want to treat the last book of the Bible as though it is a prophetic jigsaw puzzle, written to be solved for the terminal generation of Christians. Others dismiss it as being too veiled, too complex, and too culture bound to benefit modern believers. And still others so spiritualize the text, they render it as little more than a book of parables and allegories.

In the early years of my life in Christ I was exposed to a very detailed analysis of Revelation. I was grilled to believe that anyone who really took God's Word seriously and literally would adopt this interpretation, and all the charts that came with it. I was assured that it was the oldest and, therefore, the most trustworthy. All other attempts at explaining Revelation were labeled as being either from a theologically "liberal" tradition or of too recent a vintage to be taken seriously.

This particular school of interpretation led me and many of my young Christian friends to develop some wrong thinking and wrong habits. I found myself spending too much time reading the headlines and listening to the latest news reports in order to interpret biblical prophecy. (I am still trying to find those Vietcong helicopters in the text!) I was too taken up with "end times" sensationalism. Instead, I needed to develop a biblical worldview—to be so grounded in the Scriptures, I could view all of life from God's perspective.

Looking back I can also see where this interpretation of Revelation made me far more aware of Satan and the pervasiveness of evil than of the sovereignty of God, who rules over all from His throne in heaven, and the triumphant Lamb of God, who "came to destroy the works of the devil." I withdrew from my culture out of fear into the "safety" of an ingrown Christian subculture. It grieves me to reflect upon how uninvolved and detached I was from the secular world, but this Christian-cocoon living was actually encouraged. We called it "community."

Lastly, this teaching on Revelation prompted me to develop a privatized and individualized spirituality. I had very little understanding of the importance of the Church and our corporate life as the people of God. I remember a whole lot of emphasis on being an "overcomer" through discipline and "trying harder" to please God and much less about trusting boldly in Jesus and in His all-sufficient grace. Since I am a proud man who loves to perform, I became a Pharisee among Pharisees. Today, I'm a Pharisee in recovery!

I am not sure if my anger or my pain is greater as I recount these things. I finally came to the point of giving up on the book of Revelation. It became a closed part of the Scripture. I returned to the "safe" haven of the epistles of Paul—Romans, Ephesians, Galatians. It wasn't until the people in my congregation prevailed upon me for months to offer a study of the book of Revelation (hounded is more like it!) that I dared to venture back into this part of God's Word. This time as I looked at the text for myself, doing research and cross-checking passages, I saw Revelation in a whole new light.

What a surprise our heavenly Father had in store for me as I sought to read and ponder Revelation as though I were a part of that first community of faith in Asia Minor that received John's series of visions. I have never enjoyed examining and teaching a portion of the Bible more than the year we spent working through this text. Owning both my previous ignorance and prejudices, it was wonderful to rejoice with childlike wonder at what God was opening to us through His Scriptures. In the following chapters, I will share with you what we discovered to be both true and freeing.

Now let me say at the outset that I offer nothing new or novel in this volume. An angel has not appeared to me while in the Alps to reveal secrets that no other man has ever seen. I make no claim to original thoughts or exegesis. That is both the source of my joy and my anger. I am thrilled to say and to celebrate that what you are about to read is not simply my, Scott Ward Smith's, private or esoteric interpretation! The way I will be explaining and applying the text of Revelation has many precedents throughout the history of the church! If that were not the case I would, indeed, be both crazy and presumptuous! My joy is simply in creatively restating these truths for God's people of my generation. My anger is born out of the sense of loss that I was not exposed to these great and liberating insights until much later in my life.

The Living Hope in the Book of Revelation

This brings me to my second reason for writing this book. I am driven by a heartfelt concern for the hurting and biblically hungry people of God and by their pronounced need for a real substantive hope. The older I have gotten as a Christian husband, dad, son, friend, and pastor, the more I am constrained to conclude that life is hard, very hard. I also realize how biblically ill-informed our generation of believers is to understand the Christian life—and all of life—from God's perspective. (After all, I was addicted to this same malady.)

Thankfully my own formula-based spirituality of the late '60s and '70s—with all of its principles and promises for "abundant living"—has long since faded into a more honest, if painful, understanding of the normal Christian life. The theologically thin veneer of the "name it and claim it" prosperity teaching (which also influenced me for a season) has been exposed for what it really is: The vain attempt of many Christians to tame, predict, and control the sovereign purposes of Almighty God. I no longer use "biblical Band-Aids" to cover the gaping wounds of the cancers of the human experience.

Has my youthful optimism given way to an adult pessimism? Has Tigger become Eeyore? No, not at all. It's just that a "super-spiritual" idealism has been replaced with a biblical realism—for which I thank our Father in heaven.

This is where God's good gift of hope comes in. I see a huge difference between the way we customarily think of hope and how the Bible defines the term. To the average man on the street, *hope* is a vague sense of well-being, based on the contingency that certain things work out. (We hope that we are going to have a good family vacation—which must be accompanied by certain specifications: that it does not rain, that the children cooperate, and that the fish bite and the mosquitoes don't!)

However, hope in the Scriptures is "eschatological," as biblical theologians say—pertaining to the "last things." The incomparable wonders of what is ahead for God's people are brought to bear upon our present difficult circumstances. This is why the second coming of Jesus Christ is referred to as "our blessed hope." When our Lord returns, all will be made right!

The apostle Paul expressed this hope in his letters from prison: "I consider that our present sufferings are not worth comparing with the glory that will be revealed in us . . . we . . . groan inwardly as we wait eagerly for our adoption as sons, the redemption of our bodies. For in this hope we were saved" (Rom. 8:18, 23, 24). Paul's pain was not eradicated; it was redefined by his hope. Such confidence frees Christians in every age and place to "rejoice in the hope of the glory of God" (Rom. 5:2).

The apostle Peter expressed this same hope: "In his [Jesus'] great mercy he has given us new birth into a living hope through the resurrection of Jesus Christ from the dead, and into an inheritance that can never perish, spoil or fade— kept in heaven for you, who through faith are shielded by God's power until the coming of the salvation that is ready to be revealed in the last time. In this you greatly rejoice, though now for a little while you may have had to suffer grief in all kinds of trials" (1 Pet. 1:3–6).

Hope does not replace grief and trials, it wondrously transforms them. We are led to set our "hope fully on the grace to be given [to us] when Jesus Christ is revealed" (1 Pet. 1:13).

As I worked through the text of Revelation, however, I also discovered that our present experience of hope is not just tied to our wonderful future as God's people, but also to what has happened in the past and what is going on in the present. We have a sure hope because of what Jesus accomplished in the past upon the cross as the Lamb of God. We have a living hope because of the present occupied throne of God in heaven. Indeed, our hope comes from "him who is, and who was, and who is to come" (Rev. 1:4). He is, as Peter called Him, the "God of all grace"—past grace, present grace, and future grace!

God never intended Revelation to be a source of fear and confusion. It gave rise to Handel's *Messiah*, not Mozart's *Requiem for the Dead*! Why would the last of the sixty-six books of the sacred canon be written to do anything less than bring this great encouragement and hope? It is not a

dark hidden mystery to be decoded by members of the illu-
mined deeper-life club. Rather, it is a heavenly perspective to
be seen, embraced, and rejoiced in by the hearts of those with
vivid imaginations and childlike faith. This book of overwhelming sights, nearly-audible sounds, and rich symbols is
meant to bring eternal encouragement and liberating perspective to every generation of Christians—not just to the
first-century church, facing the violent persecution of the
Roman world, or to the last-century church, facing the worst
of the final days before the coming of Jesus.

Followers of the Lamb everywhere, and in all periods of
church history, face struggles, fears, and heartaches similar
to those of the first readers of Revelation. The setting and the
circumstances vary, but spiritual warfare goes on everywhere
at every time. There have been more Christian martyrs in the
twentieth century than the combined number of martyrs in
the preceding nineteen centuries!

I personally have received more help in enduring my
everyday problems from studying Revelation than from any
other portion of God's Word in the nearly thirty years I have
been a Christian. And I have received more guidance for how
to live the Christian life and how to begin a new church from
this book than from any other. Revelation is not just a guidebook for dealing with the end times; it is a guidebook for
every day of our lives. That's what I found as I studied this
book and that's what my church found as we used these principles to guide our life together.

How Then Shall We Read?

Unveiled Hope is written with far more pastoral concerns
than academic ones! But, as I was taught as a young Christian,
"Every text without a context becomes a pretext for a proof-
text!" What, then, is the historical context of Revelation? And

what are some of the things we need to be aware of in interpreting this unique New Testament book?

Revelation opens with the claim: The Lord Jesus, Himself, is writing this book! As that is the case, I am convinced that the apostle John was the human interpreter. Jesus gave the apostle who wrote the Gospel of John and the three epistles that bear his name the honor of writing the book that closes the Bible. This same John, who was a member of the band of twelve disciples, walked with Jesus His entire itinerant ministry. Within that twelve Peter, James, and John formed a trio who were privileged to share some of the most intimate moments with our Lord, such as His Transfiguration and the agony of the Garden of Gethsemane. John himself was referred to as "the beloved disciple" who laid his head upon Jesus' breast the night He was betrayed and to whom our Lord entrusted the care of His mother, just before He died.

Is Revelation Apocalyptic Literature?

John calls his book "the revelation of Jesus Christ" (Rev. 1:1). The word *revelation* in Greek is *apokalypsis*, which means "disclosure" or "unveiling." (Thus, Mike and I call our book and his album "Unveiled Hope.") The title and the style of John's epistle have led many scholars to conclude that his book is a Christian example of a Jewish genre of literature called "apocalyptic," written between 200 B.C. and A.D. 100.

Apocalypses became popular at a time when the people of God were suffering intensely and God seemed to be silent. Israel's prophets were dead, and there was a need for a word from heaven to bring understanding and hope. In general, these writings claimed to be a message from God, given through an angelic mediator to some important figure or hero from the past (like Enoch or Moses). They used rich and enigmatic symbolism to show how God would break into history to overthrow evil. The second half of the book of Daniel is an Old Testament model for this genre.

Two opposing worlds or ages clash and create the setting for the drama of all apocalypses: God's and Satan's. Jewish apocalyptists, unlike their Persian counterparts, however, did not teach that God and Satan were equals. Rather, God created Satan and he is always subordinate to God. The present evil age is temporary and is under Satan's control. The future age, under God's direct rule, will be glorious and eternal. It will prevail over all opposition!

Apocalyptic literature is similar to our political cartoons, in which certain images are readily identifiable. For example, in our day the eagle stands for the United States; in the first century, the sea monster stood for the great enemy of God, Satan. The drama between God and Satan, the evil age and the age to come, are played out in fanciful and spectacular imagery. In the end, God always triumphs. Evil is destroyed.

If you are at all familiar with the book of Revelation, you can readily understand why many suggest that it is at least a by-product of apocalyptic literature. But there are some major differences. John is no hero from the past. He is a pastor in the present! He claims to be writing prophecy, not merely expressing good feelings about the future. The voice of God is not silent. John knows himself to be writing the very "word of God" (Rev. 1:2). And unlike other apocalyptics, John calls for moral action in the culture. He is not as "world-denying" as they are.

While apocalypses look almost exclusively to the future for deliverance, John bids us to also look to the past, in which the Lamb of God has already triumphed! The great battle has been won at Calvary! The mop-up operation is well under way. History is the unfolding of God's sovereign plan of grace and mercy for the nations of the world.

Prophecy, for John, comes to us as both a foretelling and a forth-telling. Yes, we look to the future for the full manifestation of the triumph of King Jesus. But we also live in the present with encouragement, hope, power, and purpose. Clearly Revelation bears the marks of apocalyptic literature. Yet it is primarily written to call us to live to the glory of God, right here and now, with hearts filled with His peace!

The Language and Writing Style of Revelation

John's genre and writing style is another very important issue as we prepare to interpret this unique portion of the Scriptures, full of strange images, beasts, and symbols. God commissioned him to "show his servants what must soon take place" (Rev. 1:1). The Greek word used in this phrase means to "signify" or to set forth in symbols. As John wrote the Revelation, he did so with a particular literary format in mind, which was different from the way he wrote his gospel and his three epistles.

We must be very careful, therefore, not to be overly zealous in creating visual representations or in assigning meaning to every detail in Revelation. As John Stott reminds us, "It is important to remember that the imagery he uses is intended to be symbolical rather than pictorial. The various elements in the vision are significant symbols to be interpreted, rather than actual features to be imagined."[1]

Does this mean that we are not to interpret Revelation literally? The answer depends on what we mean by *literal interpretation*. To literally interpret any portion of the Scriptures we must be careful to identify the *literary genre* of the text. The Bible contains many rich expressions of language and writing styles. God is an artist with words! He writes with many techniques—poetry, narrative, prophecy, prose, parable, history, proverb, song, didactic theology, pastoral letters, just to name a few.

Within these we also find literary devices such as onomatopoeia, assonance, simile, allegory, metaphor, alliteration, hyperbole, and acrostics. Nothing about the Bible is bland or boring! To "rightly divide the word of truth" we must learn the appropriate rules for recognizing, reading, and interpreting each of these techniques. This requires hard work, but the benefits far outweigh the effort. The history of the Church is littered with the consequences of God's people failing to interpret the text of God's Word according to sound principles of biblical exegesis.

For example, we would do well to learn a lesson from the Jews of the first century whose expectations of a political deliverer completely overshadowed any understanding of the Messiah who would come, first of all, to die for the sins of God's people. We must be very careful not to repeat their mistake in our zeal to predict the nature and timing of our Lord's second coming. I learned a long time ago that prophecy is best interpreted by its own fulfillment! Enough is made patently clear in the Bible to keep us busy until the less clear is made providentially certain.

The Numbers Game

We also want to give special attention to certain numbers in the book of Revelation. As you read through the text you will find reoccurring expressions of four, seven, ten, and twelve—and multiples of these. Pastor and scholar Michael Wilcock counsels us that, "Numbers are much more likely to be symbols than statistics. And these symbolic number patterns clearly have great importance, or the drama would not include such a lot of them."[2]

Take the number *seven* for an example. Six clearly defined series of *sevens* run through Revelation:

1. The Seven Churches (Rev. 2:1–3:22)
2. The Seven Seals (Rev. 4:1–8:1)
3. The Seven Trumpets (Rev. 8:2–11:19)
4. The Seven Signs in Heaven (Rev. 12:1–15:8)
5. The Seven Bowls of Wrath (Rev. 16:1–21)
6. The Seven Final Visions (Rev. 17:1–22:21)

And a seventh series of seven is in Rev. 10:4, the "seven thunders," which John was told not to reveal, but to seal. Perhaps this is one of God's ways of reminding us that the visions of Revelation are not exhaustive. There is still much that we do not and cannot know about God's providential orderings and dealings.

The number *seven* first appears in the Bible in the opening pages of Genesis. God establishes this seven-beat rhythm when He creates the world in six days and then rests on the seventh. *Seven* becomes a pattern, which reoccurs many other times in the Scriptures, "especially thickly in the chapters which describe Old Testament religion—days and years, altars and sacrificial animals, sprinklings of water and oil and blood, again and again in groups of seven."[3] Commentators have suggested, therefore, that the number *seven* represents concepts like completeness, perfection, or reality.

It will be important for us to interpret the other main numbers found in Revelation with an open Old Testament as well. Some of these numbers are rich with significance and symbolism. We want to be careful, however, to guard against the extremes of "mathematical exegesis," which is just another form of treating Revelation like a puzzle. There have been some very complex and fanciful interpretations of the Apocalypse based on decoding the numerics. Such treatments have at times shown utter disregard for the clear meaning and intent of the text.

Revelation Baggage

So how are we to interpret this unique book of visions, pastoral instruction, and prophecy? It is very important that we recognize any baggage that each of us brings to our study of Revelation. No other book in the Bible has suffered more at the hands of prejudice and presupposition than this one. Martin Luther once wryly commented, "Everyone thinks of the book whatever his spirit imparts."[4]

Let's look at the four main schools of interpretation represented by evangelical Bible scholars. First, the *preterist school*, which holds that Revelation is written in veiled language, almost exclusively about events in John's own time. This is also sometimes referred to as the "Roman view," emphasizing that the symbols and situations are to be understood in light of the growing persecution of Christians by Rome. The drama of Revelation is seen as culminating with the overthrow and destruction of the Roman empire.

The *futurist view*, also known as the "second coming" view, is by far the most popular position, and is held by most contemporary evangelical interpreters. It stresses that Revelation is primarily a book of prophecies of events yet to come, especially of events that immediately precede the second coming of Jesus Christ.

The *historicist view* sees the text as a charting of the complete history of the Church between the two comings of Christ. Though the specifics vary by those who hold to this schema, each period of church history is relegated to a section of Revelation. Thus, this position is also referred to as the "church history" view.

The *idealist view* teaches that Revelation contains principles applicable for Christians in every generation.

Each of these four positions is championed by those with the highest regard for the Scriptures, believers who affirm that the Bible is without error in all that it teaches. I believe we can gain valuable insights from all of them; we don't need to embrace one of these schools of interpretation to the exclusion of the other three.

I also encourage each of us to be careful of our preconceived notions and stereotypes as we approach the difficult issue of the millennium, the thousand-year reign of Christ in Revelation 20. What would the recipients of John's letter have understood by this image, which is mentioned specifically only once in the entire Bible? Is John writing about a literal reign of Jesus upon the earth? And if so, will the second coming of our Lord occur at the beginning of this period? (Our "premillennial" friends insist that Jesus will return bodily to our world before the beginning of the thousand years.) Or are we to anticipate His return at the end of this wonderful period of gospel advancement among the nations, as our "postmillennial" ("post" meaning after) friends encourage us to believe? Or is this, as many have suggested, a reference to a "spiritual" reign of our Lord, one that is going on right now (the "amillennial" view)? (The *a* prefix is not meant to imply that there will be no millennium, but rather that there will not be an earthly or materialistic reign of Jesus prior to the end of history as we know it.) Sound confusing? You bet it is.

Christians have drawn swords in their defense of their millennial position. So who's right?

We will study the issues surrounding this thousand-year reign of Jesus later in the book, but it is important to recognize that men and women who have died in service of the Lamb of God have embraced each of the historic positions on the millennium (premillennial, postmillennial, and amillennial). If nothing else, this should caution each of us to avoid the temptation of being overly simplistic and dogmatic about such matters. One's position on the millennium is not simply a matter of a conservative versus a liberal interpretation of the Bible. Failure to realize this has led to many unnecessary divisions among Christians.

So how are we to work through the quagmire of opinions surrounding the interpretation of Revelation?

On Our Faces . . . and As Children

The best way to come to the text of the closing book of the Bible is to prostrate ourselves before the One it so clearly reveals. We can learn a valuable lesson from John's experience as he received his first vision of several visions, a vision of the exalted Jesus. When he saw our Lord, in all of His glory and grace, John fell at His feet as a dead man. Such reverence, awe, and brokenness are becoming to those who ponder what is taught in Revelation, or, for that matter, what is taught in any of the Scriptures. Right now we all only "know in part." "Then (when Jesus returns) we shall know fully." Until "then," may our textual and theological confidence be adorned with the appropriate humility!

Neither Mike Card nor myself purport to offer a detailed exegesis and explanation of every verse in the book of Revelation. (For those of you desiring a more comprehensive treatment of the text, refer to the bibliography in the appendix.) Our goal, rather, is to offer a thematic exposition, one that traces the theme of hope as it is revealed in each section of John's letter. Sometimes our study will involve meditating on a whole chapter. At other times we will look at a few chapters as a unit or just one verse as we seek to demonstrate the eternal encouragement of Revelation.

Finally let me offer a suggestion I learned only a few years ago from an evangelical New Testament scholar who teaches at a seminary in the northeast. Read Revelation with the heart of a child. More than once Jesus held up a child to His disciples as a model of kingdom faith and trust. As we get older, the "hardening of the categories" tends to set in and most of us are not as given to the "living and breathing" character of the Bible. But only children can discern some things through their unspoiled senses and awesome capacity to see with their souls. Ask your heavenly Father to quicken the imagination with which He endowed you at birth, and try to enter into the sights and sounds that John has recorded. Do not get bogged down and agonize over trying to find or to assign a meaning to every detail in the text. There is enough that is patently clear in Revelation to keep us busy until Jesus returns!

The Hope to Come

The sights, the smells, the tastes, and the sounds of this little village in Switzerland stir and intensify within me my longings and anticipation as I ponder the fulfillment of our great hope. If the "new heavens and the new earth" look no different from what I experience sitting here on the balcony of Hotel Garni Edelweiss, then I am a satisfied son of the living God. And yet the Scriptures teach us that no eye has seen, nor ear has heard, nor has the thought ever entered into the mind of man what God has in store for His people (1 Cor. 2:9). I meditate upon these words and I cry out with my brothers and sisters in every age the prayer offered in the last paragraph of Revelation, "Even so, come, Lord Jesus!" (Rev. 22:20 KJV).

CHAPTER ONE

REVELATION 1
A VISION OF JESUS:
THE FOUNDATION OF ALL HOPE

FROM THE WORD

The first book I read after becoming a Christian in 1968 was J. B. Phillips's little volume *Your God Is Too Small*. Written in the mid-'60s, it offered an exposé of what the citizens of Great Britain really thought of God, versus what they professed Him to be in the creeds they recited each Lord's Day. Dr. Phillips's premise was simple: The most important thing about any of us is the image of God we carry in our hearts, for the quality of our lives is determined by the way we think of Him.

I do not think it too strong or simplistic to suggest that this is also the main purpose of the book of Revelation. Beginning boldly in chapter 1 and gaining momentum through chapter 22, Revelation is primarily a revelation of Jesus Christ. As Eugene Peterson, Professor of Pastoral Ministry and Spiritual Formation at Regent College in Vancouver, British Columbia, commented, "The Revelation gives us the last word on Christ, and the word is that Christ is center and at the center. Without this controlling center, the Bible is a mere encyclopedia of religion with no more plot than a telephone directory."[1]

How appropriate it is, then, for God to conclude His written Word with a comprehensive and consuming presentation of the magnificence of His Son. Throughout John's pastoral prophecy, Jesus is "unveiled": He is made known in all of His glory and grace. What we think of Him matters more than anything. "The essence of idolatry," said A. W. Tozer, "is the entertainment of thoughts about God that are unworthy of Him."[2] John writes to decry and to destroy all such false images.

As a child, the first concepts of Jesus that filled my heart did not come from the Scriptures, but from the pictures in the Sunday School and Vacation Bible School curriculum. Jesus never seemed to be looking at me. He was always turned a little bit to the side, looking off into the distance, usually with a little lamb draped over His shoulders. His beautiful light brown hair, with its brilliant sheen and wavy locks, resembled the Breck Girl of the shampoo commercials I had seen on TV and on the back of my mother's magazines. His fair complexion and rosy cheeks had an air-brushed aura. I had a hard time believing that this guy spent very much time at a carpenter's bench or even outside in the Judean sun! I also thought it strange that He never had any wrinkles in His linen garments. Did He always stand up? (Maybe the disciples had a portable steamer!)

From Jesus the Breck Girl I graduated to Jesus the big screen, mono-dimensional movie character. Why was it that He never laughed or even smiled in these films? Jesus always seemed to be in some drug-induced state. With glazed-over eyes, He lacked passion and always seemed to be reciting a script. There was nothing natural about the way He conversed with people, even with His own disciples, who were also depicted as a rather dull bunch.

Despite this bad art, I became a Christian just before my undergraduate studies. One of the first things I did before moving into my dorm room was to buy a print of a painting of Jesus created by the artist Frances Hook. Finally, I had found what I considered to be a great representation of our Lord! He had a ruddy face with uncombed hair. His clothes looked like they had been slept in. A wry smile defined His revolutionary expression. He was still looking off into the distance but that didn't matter. I had found a late-'60s Jesus! Even before they met me, my two freshman roommates saw this framed painting propped up on my bed. They assumed it was a portrait of Che Guiverra or some other radical communist liberator and were only somewhat relieved to learn it was a picture of Jesus!

Now, after many years of studying the Scriptures and getting to know our Lord as He is represented there, I understand why some of the Reformers railed against the sixteenth-century religious art in Western Europe. For them, it was a matter of obedience to the first two of the Ten Commandments—"You shall have no other gods before me" and "You shall not make for yourself any idol." For me, it is also a matter of the power of bad art to influence our understanding of God.

Some fifty years before John wrote Revelation, Jesus asked him and the rest of the twelve disciples, "Who do you say I am?" (Matt. 16:15). This question stays before each of us, Christians and non-Christians alike. I constantly resist the temptation to reshape Jesus into a more predictable, manageable, and accommodating deity. More often than not, I want a masseuse, not a Master!

No other book in the Bible gives us a more inviting and overwhelming picture of Jesus. Here is Jesus as He really is. Jesus, as He wants to be known. Jesus, who alone is worthy of our adoration, our affection, and our allegiance. As we trace the theme of hope throughout John's visions we will see that Jesus Himself is the foundation of our abiding hope. He is the reason why we do not ultimately despair.

This is why the author of the book of Hebrews bids us to look to "fix our eyes on Jesus, the author and perfecter of our faith, who for the joy set before him endured the cross, scorning its shame, and sat down at the right hand of the throne of God. Consider him who endured such opposition from sinful men, so that you will not grow weary and lose heart" (Heb. 12:2–3). This very hope filled the heart of the author of Revelation.

John Begins His Writing

John, the aged apostle, is in an involuntary exile for "the word of God and the testimony of Jesus Christ." He is on the island of Patmos in the Aegean Sea, about thirty-seven miles west-southwest of Asia Minor. Sixty square miles of rocks and mountains become the pulpit from which he shares the words and visions that God gives him for the church.

At this moment the people of God and the world are involved in a deadly conflict. Intense spiritual warfare is escalating. Persecution is no longer occasional and local, but regular and widespread. Rome's satanic attacks are not, however, the only peril the church is facing.

Heresy, immorality, and worldliness are within her gates. Distortions of the gospel, powerful false teachers, sexual enticement, the lure of cultural acceptance and financial success—all these are affecting the church, even before the dawn of the second century. John writes of a Sovereign Lord and a Savior Lamb at such a time and to such a people.

Let's look at how he begins:

The revelation of Jesus Christ, which God gave him to
show his servants what must soon take place. He made it

known by sending his angel to his servant John, who testifies to everything he saw—that is, the word of God and
the testimony of Jesus Christ. Blessed is the one who reads
the words of this prophecy, and blessed are those who
hear it and take to heart what is written in it, because the
time is near. (1:1–3)

In these opening verses of chapter 1, John makes it clear
that he writes neither as a social commentator, nor as an
inspired pastor, nor as an ecstatic seer. He is conscious of
writing the very words and pictures that God gives him. One
of the greatest joys and one of the most sobering realities in
the Christian life is to realize that we serve a God who has
chosen to reveal Himself and to give us His written Word. As
J. I. Packer, Professor of Systematic and Historical Theology
at Regent College in Vancouver, British Columbia, once said
when I heard him lecture while in seminary, "God has spoken and He has not stuttered." Because God continues to
speak to us through the Scriptures, we can have real peace
and concrete assurance.

It is important to note the beatitude or blessing with
which John begins this last installment in the canon of
God's Word: "Blessed is the one who reads the words of this
prophecy, and blessed are those who hear it and take to heart
what is written in it, because the time is near" (vs. 3). Revelation is not written to amuse us, but to transform us.

John's Audience and Revelation's Date

John writes to Christians in seven real churches in Asia
Minor (modern-day Turkey), all within a ninety-mile radius
of each other. It has been several decades since Jesus was
raised from the dead. There is no real consensus, but most
scholars agree that Revelation was written either at the end

of Nero's reign (A.D. 54–68) or during Vespasian's (A.D. 69–79). Still others favor a date in the later years of Domitian's reign of terror (A.D. 81–96). I am inclined to go with this later date.

Politically, persecution of Christians is clearly spreading. The aging apostle is writing from a Roman penal colony on Patmos, a little island off the coast of Asia where he is in exile against his will. In all probability, John was sent there as punishment for being a leader in the early church. Such actions would be considered a threat to the order and honor of the Roman Empire.

The Roman emperor is demanding that he be worshiped as a god. To fail to acknowledge "Caesar as Lord" by offering a pinch of incense to the emperor's guardian spirit imperils not just one's home and job, but one's life. The recipients of John's letter are living under this constant threat.

Spiritually, many churches are beginning to be influenced by the "good life" and by bad theology. Other fellowships are beginning to wonder about the "hope of His coming." From without and from within, the young church is in a time of crisis.

Each of these local assemblies was to read John's circular letter aloud. Nothing in his visionary epistle was irrelevant to those hearing these words for the first time. I will emphasize this point over and over. John wrote every word, symbol, and image to encourage and to prepare them for life in the hostile Roman world. This is true of the prophetic material John recorded as well. Promises of "future grace" bring present hope and strength. As the writer of Hebrews has said, "Now faith is being sure of what we hope for and certain of what we do not see" (Heb. 11:1).

The context of John's writing must be remembered if we are to guard against unhinged and fanciful futuristic interpretations of the book. Nothing in Revelation is irrelevant to the first-century church. Every vision, every prophecy, every exhortation, every promise, and every warning is written with them in mind. Unfortunately, many commentaries and expositions of John's words and visions do not make this point primary to their interpretation. Some actually teach that after the letters to the churches, which end in chapter 5, the church is not even mentioned until the end of the book. This interpretation deprives many Christians of Revelation's power to encourage them and minimizes the book's relevancy for the universal church.

The joy and focus of John's initial greeting sets the tone for his whole composition. He prays that "grace and peace" will be the feast of all who receive the words of this prophecy (1:4). The gift of God's grace always precedes our experience of His peace. It is the "incomparable riches of his grace, expressed in his kindness to us in Christ Jesus" (Eph. 2:7) that leads to a peace "which passes all understanding."

We Would See Jesus

John credits each member of the Trinity as being the source of these great blessings. He speaks of God the Father as "him who is, and who was, and who is to come" (vs. 4). Our God is eternal! The Holy Spirit is referred to as "the seven spirits before his throne." This unique phrase can also be translated "the sevenfold Spirit." In either case, this is the first of many uses of the number *seven* in Revelation.

Finally he mentions Jesus, which is unusual in our customary ordering of the members of the Trinity; John does so because he is going to primarily focus on Jesus' person and work throughout the letter. This is a "revelation of Jesus Christ"—from Him and of Him! John writes with a thoroughgoing Christocentricity. The apostle Paul shared this same conviction. It is God's will, he said, "when the times will have reached their fulfillment—to bring all things in heaven and on earth together under one head, even Christ" (Eph. 1:10).

What does John, the beloved apostle, a pastor whose heart could easily be overwhelmed and broken in light of the current events, need as he is cut off from the rich fellowship of God's people? What do the Christians under his care in Asia Minor need more than anything else, as they are feeling the heat and hatred of the Roman world? What have all Christians needed during the past twenty centuries as they have confronted the many challenges that are a part of our journey of faith? Jesus!

John Stott, Rector Emeritis of All Souls Church in London, England, put it brilliantly: We do not need "a detailed forecast of future events which has to be laboriously deciphered, but (rather) a vision of Jesus Christ, to cheer the faint and encourage the weary. John's desire is not to satisfy our curiosity about the future but to stimulate our faithfulness in the present."[3] He is writing to encourage—not to confound!

To see Jesus is to have hope, for as the apostle Paul stated, Christ Himself is our hope (1 Tim. 1:1). And so it is for all Christians. Peter looked upon Jesus, instead of the tossing waves, and he was not swallowed by the stormy sea. Stephen looked up and saw Jesus "standing at the right hand of God," and had the courage and power to pray for those who were stoning him to death (Acts 7). Yet I can only savor the freedom and peace, which Jesus alone can bring, when I am far more preoccupied with our Lord than with my circumstances and my petty little self-serving agenda. As I read and meditate through Revelation, I become more certain that John is basically asserting that the main issue in life is: "How big and how good is your Jesus?"

And John now describes the Jesus he knows.

26

A Portrait of Praise

John's first description of Jesus is a portrait of praise. Jesus is "the ruler of the kings of the earth" (1:5). Caesar is not Lord, Jesus is! Can you imagine the high praise that probably broke out as this statement was read for the first time in the churches in Asia Minor? Christ is to be worshiped, not Emperor Domitian. Every generation of Christians needs to be reminded that our God reigns. The sovereignty of God, just like the grace of God, is a major theme that permeates all twenty-two chapters of Revelation. Our Lord has no rivals. All of His enemies will be overthrown. He who sits enthroned in heaven laughs and mocks at the futile attempts of little kings to contend with the King of Kings and Lord of Lords (Ps. 2). The people of God do not need to be paralyzed with fear as they live in a hostile world, even when they face martyrdom in the Colosseum of Rome. Our God has installed His King. He will prevail.

The best-known Christian chorus goes like this, "Jesus loves me this I know, for the Bible tells me so . . ." Though this great truth is implicit in the whole of Scriptures, it is made explicit here in John's opening word of praise. "To him who loves us and has freed us from our sins by his blood . . ." (vs. 5). Jesus loves us! Present tense. Actively, passionately, perfectly, completely—forever!

At this point John's theology becomes his doxology! He bids the persecuted Christians of Asia Minor in the last decade of the first century—and us—to join him in a sacrifice of praise, for we are a "kingdom and priests" (1:6). Every Christian has both the privilege of intimate access into the presence of God and the calling to represent God to the world. Is it any wonder that John cries out, ". . . to him be glory and power forever and ever! Amen" (vs. 6)?

When I came to this section the first evening of our

27

church's study of Revelation, I saw the eyes of my good friends in our fellowship light up. Suddenly, it occurred to all of us that our lives really do matter to God. What a profound calling we have as the beloved of the Lord to live as a "kingdom of priests"! Unfortunately, all too often our identity is defined by what we do to pay the bills as opposed to our vocation as the people of God. From that moment on in our study joy, rather than fear, became the predominant emotion that dominated our weekly gatherings.

As John ponders this love, he cannot help but think of the time when this outpouring of grace will be perfected in us. He who loves us is coming back for us! "Look, he is coming with the clouds, / and every eye will see him . . ." (1:7). This time, however, He will come, not on the back of a colt, but on clouds of glory. All "peoples of the earth" will be affected. All. Those who have received His grace, which flows so freely from the cross, will experience unspeakable joy; for our sins (which fixed Jesus to His tree of death no less than did the nails) have been forgiven—all of them! Those who have rejected His amazing love will experience unparalleled mourning. "So shall it be! Amen."

Visions in the Spirit

John continues to bid us to rivet our gaze on Jesus as he records the first of many visions God gave him. In simple humility he refers to himself as John, "your brother and companion in the suffering and kingdom and patient endurance that are ours in Jesus" (1:9). These words remind us that we are in union with our Lord and with each other. This is the essence of community. As members of God's kingdom we are not shielded from hardship. Rather, "we must go through many hardships to enter the kingdom of

God" (Acts 14:22). The good news is that He is with us; therefore, we patiently endure.

Jesus spoke to John with trumpet-like clarity and instructed him to write "what you see" (1:11). Upon hearing this clarion call, John turns to see the One speaking to him, and he is overwhelmed with magnificent sights and sounds:

> I turned around to see the voice that was speaking to me. And when I turned I saw seven golden lampstands, and among the lampstands was someone "like a son of man," dressed in a robe reaching down to his feet and with a golden sash around his chest. His head and hair were white like wool, as white as snow, and his eyes were like blazing fire. His feet were like bronze glowing in a furnace, and his voice was like the sound of rushing waters. In his right hand he held seven stars, and out of his mouth came a sharp double-edged sword. His face was like the sun shining in all its brilliance. (1:12–16)

Doesn't sound much like that Breck Girl Jesus or that monodimensional movie character. This picture is closer to Che Giuverra. Yet the first thing that catches John's attention in this vision is Jesus standing *in the midst of his people*, the "seven golden lampstands" (1:20). As Bruce Metzger, Professor of New Testament and Textual Criticism at Princeton Theological Seminary, Princeton, New Jersey, has said, "Christ is not an absentee landlord."[4] He is with us and He is for us. He is our Immanuel. John goes on to describe Jesus in rich imagery and symbolism that is not meant to be painted, but rather to be pondered.

The beloved apostle's heart was filled with Old Testament revelation and with an understanding of the whole Messianic tradition. Of the 404 verses that constitute the twenty-two chapters of Revelation, 278 of them contain at least one allusion to an Old Testament passage! We dare not miss this point. *John's only* code language *is that of God's Word!*

The "Son of Man" in John's vision is none other than the glorious persona described by the same name in Daniel 7:13. (Jesus used this title more than any other when referring to Himself during His public ministry.) Deliverance from the Babylonian captivity was just a foreshadowing of the deliverance from sin that Jesus would win for His people in fulfilling Daniel's prophecy.

John sees Jesus clothed with the robe, perhaps representative of both a king and a high priest. Jesus, the King of Kings and the Lord of Lords. Jesus, the great, faithful, and merciful high priest presiding over a throne of grace for the people of God. The "golden sash" around His chest further speaks of His royal authority (Ex. 28:8; 39:5). The "white hair" adorning His head is not an expression of age but of wisdom and of the respect due Him (Dan. 7:9; Prov. 16:31). This is none other than Daniel's "Ancient of Days"! The penetrating scrutiny of our Lord is symbolized by His "eyes of blazing fire." His stability and strength are emphasized by His "feet like glowing brass." Tom Howard, Professor of English at Gordon College in South Hamilton, Mississippi, correctly observes, this is not "a pale Galilean, but a towering and furious figure who will not be managed."[5]

John describes the voice he hears as having the might and authority of "rushing waters," the very expression Ezekiel used to describe the voice of God (Ezek. 1:24; 43:2). In Jesus' right hand are the "seven stars," which John tells us represent the angels or messengers of the seven churches. Once again we are given a picture of the involvement and care that our Lord gives to His people (1:20). The "double-edged sword" that issues from his mouth is certainly metaphorical and not metaphysical! Jesus' words are true and powerful. He speaks grace for His people and destruction for His enemies (Isa. 11:4; Heb.

4:12). Lastly, the face of Jesus is seen in all of its overwhelming brilliance: "like the sun," His glory shines forth.

John had encountered this glory previously on the Mount of Transfiguration (Matt. 17:2). He had also been with Jesus in His resurrection state. But now he is given an even fuller revelation of the glorified Son and, appropriately, John is undone. He falls down as a dead man at the feet of Jesus. This is a true "slaying in the Spirit." Contrary to the contemporary phenomenon of the same name, this is no "neat experience to be sought after"; rather, it is a transforming encounter with the majesty of our Lord. We should long for such reverence and awe for the Lord Jesus to define what we call contemporary worship. But the purpose of this vision is not to leave John as a dead man, but to bring fresh life to his whole being and to give him assurance and hope as he confronts the crisis of his day.

The hand of grace touches John as he hears great words of encouragement: "Do not be afraid." That is all we need to hear from Jesus. "Do not be afraid." This refrain echoes throughout the book of Revelation. John heard Jesus utter this same phrase late one stormy night on the Sea of Galilee. The result was the quelling of a storm as a worship service broke out in a little boat (Matt. 14:25–33). Jesus can release us from our fears and effect such a calm because of who He is. He has conquered death through His resurrection and He is forever the "Living One," for He is also the source of all created life (John 1:1–3).

Jesus, and no one else, "holds the keys of Death and Hades." The final manifestation of this authority will be seen when He casts Death and Hades, themselves, into the lake of fire (Rev. 20:11–15). This will represent the death of Death itself! (1 Cor. 15)

The visions that God gives John are sufficient, but partial. It will be only when Jesus returns that we will "know fully even as we are fully known." But our confidence and our hope are bound up with the promise that these things "must soon take place" (1:1). History is moving inexorably toward God's determined end. Because this is true, as Die-trich Bonhoeffer, German pastor and Christian martyr during Hitler's Nazi regime, expressed, "We live each day as if it were our last, and each day as if there was a great future because of Jesus Christ."[6]

The word *must* in verse 1 is gigantic in its implications. There are no contingency plans in heaven. No mere probabilities; no plan B; no bail-out clauses. Everything is assured. This is neither fate nor karma. This is King Jesus who not only holds the "stars" and walks among the "lampstands," but also before whom one day every knee is going to bow and every tongue is going to confess that He is Lord, to the glory of God. In the remaining twenty-one chapters of Revelation all of these titles and images of Jesus, and more, are brought to life.

THE UNVEILING

Revelation 1:1

The revelation of Jesus Christ, which God gave him to show his servants what must soon take place. He made it known by sending his angel to his servant John . . .

FROM THE SONG

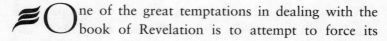

One of the great temptations in dealing with the book of Revelation is to attempt to force its immense message into the confines of a single idea. *Reductionism* it is called.

As John writes to comfort his first-century congregation who are looking persecution squarely in the face, he also writes to us today, who are squarely looking at the death of Christendom. John speaks on many levels, as does all of Scripture. Understanding his purpose in writing is not a matter of decoding or solving some complex mystery as much as it is a matter of simply listening to the Spirit. As with all Scripture, the purpose is to turn a reading eye into a listening ear.

As I seek to listen to the Spirit of the text, I am drawn again and again to a single moment that John seeks to put before me, the moment that he tells and retells from different angels at different points in the narrative. I would call it the moment of the Unveiling. Simply said, it is the moment when Jesus is revealed—the moment He appears in the clouds, the instant He comes pounding toward us astride the white warhorse, the very "twinkling of an eye" when we see Him crowned with many crowns. But more specifically for me it is the split second of realization that the Return is actually happening. The instant when you and I look up and see the reality of the Coming of Christ.

Use your imagination (that is what John's language demands). Put yourself in the then and there of the moment (for that is what John is making you do). Ask yourself where you might be. What you will be doing? Will you hear the sound of the trumpet and look out your office window?

"Did you hear something?" you will ask someone sitting next to you. Imagine for a moment what you will see.

What will it feel like to realize fully what is happening to you and the rest of the world? "So, it has all been true after all," you will whisper to yourself.

John wants to us to savor that split second. That precious

moment will not be wasted in deciphering (Oh, the locusts aren't B-52s!). It will be a moment when the Bible says Jesus—not the signs—will be "marveled at by those who believe." The moment when all we ever hoped for will be unveiled and we shall see Him at last!

"Pie in the sky?" Not at all. For it is an idea that should manifest itself in every present moment. It is an idea that transformed the quarry at Patmos, where John was literally choking to death on the marble dust, into a sanctuary, where John worshiped his once-and-future King.

This is not a notion for some far-off time but for this very moment. And if it shall be true, how must you and I live our lives in the sacrament of this present moment? If, indeed, we will one day "look up" and finally see our hope unveiled in Christ Jesus, then how must we treat our sisters and brothers now?

The Two Great Promises

The first great promise was, of course, fulfilled at His first coming, the Incarnation—a perfect promise perfectly kept, like all God's promises. Now, in the midst of the hopelessness of this first-century community—and into the midst of our own hopeless twentieth century—God speaks the second great promise.

The heart of the book of Revelation, and indeed the heart of the whole of Scripture, is the fulfillment of this promise. And here at the outset of his unveiling of the vision of Christ, John gives us that great second promise: "Behold I am coming," says Jesus. One of the uniquely comforting features of this prophecy (and prophecy is not usually so comforting) is that not only will John hear this promise, but in his vision he will actually witness its fulfillment.

The Revelation is unique in this. John has already witnessed the fulfillment of the hope about which he writes. So John sees and hears the promise; then he speaks it to those who are commanded simply to "look up." And that is to be the essence of our lives—our posture from now until He comes. We are to keep our eyes faithfully fixed "up," looking and longing for the unveiling of Jesus.

The Unveiling

Hear the roaring at the rim of the world.
See what every eye shall see.
Behold He's coming with the clouds
To set all the captives free.
And all those who longed to see this day
Will tremble with delight
As a sea of upturned faces there
Is bathed in endless Light.

I am the Alpha
And the Omega,
The One who is
And was and is to come.
Though I was dead
Now I'm alive forever.
Don't be afraid.
I hold the keys
And I have come.

Once the just and gentle Victim
Who it seemed was born to die,
See Him now, a blaze of glory
As He moves across the sky.
And that majestic silhouette
Who's come to take His bride

Still bears the healing wounds
Upon His hands and feet and side.
The great unveiling of our hope
The promised Jubilee
The revelation of our God
It's all we longed to see.

CHAPTER TWO

REVELATION 2-3
JESUS AND HIS BRIDE:
HOPE FOR THE CHURCH

FROM THE WORD

The loving and persistent prodding that led me to write this book actually goes back ten years to the summer of 1986. During those three months, the birthing of a new church—which would be centered in the beautiful community of Franklin, Tennessee, some ten miles south of Nashville—was underway. And like most births, this one was not without surprise and travail!

In the fall of 1985 my wife and I had joined with five other couples to form a "Marriage Builders Small Group." Our purpose in meeting was to reflect on our marriages through Bible study, encouragement, and prayer. Mike and Sue Card were a part of this fellowship, which embraced the importance of our walking together in community with a commitment to "bear one another's burdens" and to "provoke one another unto love and good deeds." Little did we realize the greater plan our Father had for this little group.

At the time I was serving as pastor of adult discipleship in a church in Nashville. I had been with this outstanding body of believers since its inception in 1981. One day, quite unexpectedly, the senior pastor approached me about becoming pastor for the first of several daughter churches. *Ambivalence* is the word that best describes my initial reaction to his overture. Part of me was thrilled at the prospect of being involved with building a brand new church. *Now is my chance to have the church I have always dreamed of!* I said to myself. On the other hand, a part of my heart was immediately filled with suspicion, hurt, and insecurities. *Are they just trying to get rid of me around here? What if I plant a church and it fails? What if no one even shows up?* This small group of couples proved to be the perfect setting in which to deal with my dreams and my fears in light of God's providence.

After months of wrestling and prayer, talking with my mentors, examining my heart, and searching my motives, Mike Card made one physical gesture that sealed the calling for me. He simply struck the posture of a carpenter with a saw in hand and began rocking that imaginary tool back and forth, back and forth. My heart said, *It's time to build.* No angel balanced on the bow of that unseen saw. I didn't hear a heavenly chorus break out in triumphant shouting and singing, but I did experience the peace of God, a peace that I have not doubted since we entered the whole painfully joyous process of planting a new church.

It is interesting to note that among those five other couples are Mike Card, who is a principal teacher in our church; Scott Roley, one of our pastors; and Buddy Green, an elder and worship leader. When our small group began meeting, none of us would have ever thought . . . Chalk one up for the sovereignty of God!

So how does one birth a church? Several ways—both redemptive ones and disastrous ones! With the counsel of our mother church, we invited interested families to meet with us in a Sunday school class format in the summer of 1986 to hear and pray about our vision for Franklin. To free us from our own agendas and to focus us on the heart of the Father for this new church in embryo, I led the hundred or so interested inquirers through a study of Revelation 2 and 3. That Bible study not only proved to be a wonderful way of communicating a vision for a new church, but it also led to my teaching through the entire book of Revelation some seven years later. That's how long it took me to get over my own "Revelation baggage!"

Our Father did a major work of grace in our hearts in those formative days, as most of us were coming from a variety of painful backgrounds and church experiences. And any time a new church is being formed, "Watch out!" for you will find men and women—and dogs and ponies—coming out of the woodwork to "finally have the church of their dreams."

Therefore, the initial weeks of shaping the vision for a young congregation are so critical. A church, like anything else, can simply become one more self-serving idol. This is why we began Christ Community by asking the most basic of all questions:

- What does Jesus want for His church?
- What can we learn from the Scriptures concerning His purpose, His passion, and His priorities for His people as they seek to live for His glory?
- What is to distinguish the church from every other human institution?
- What is the difference between the design for a local church found in the Bible versus what we find in our Southern culture?

What we learned during those three months of meditating on Revelation 2 and 3 still represents the "meat and taters" of our fellowship. We often return to these chapters of Revelation as a church family, for it was here that we first saw so clearly that Jesus is passionately in love with His people, the church. And when we finally studied the whole book of Revelation we discovered that every chapter and every verse resonates with this love. Our Lord is preparing a bride to love, to marry, and to cherish forever. Can you believe that this bride is you and me?

No people is more loved, right now, than the church of Jesus Christ! Grace abounds to you and me, because our Divine Bridegroom has triumphed over sin and death. We are clothed in His righteousness and are completely forgiven of all of our sins—past, present, and future. We can do *nothing* to cause Jesus to love us more than He already does. And we can do *nothing* to cause Him to love us less. We are the perfectly loved "wife of the Lamb."

Just think what such a love means, just in the human terms of the relationship between a bridegroom and his bride.

Here Comes the Bridegroom!

As a pastor I have had the privilege of officiating at many weddings, but one in particular stands out. We were at the anxiously awaited, sweaty-palms, lump-in-the-throat moment in the service when the bride was to enter. Loud and majestic strains of "Joyful, Joyful, We Adore Thee" filled the sanctuary. The doors at the back of the worship center were opened, and there she was, the bride, as ready and as beautiful as any I have ever seen (except for my wife, of course).

None of us was prepared for what happened next. Suddenly the bridegroom let out a spontaneous, "Wow!" and took off up the aisle to receive his bride! He was simply overwhelmed at the impact of the moment. I had to go after him and physically pull him back into place!

Could Jesus feel that same anticipation and excitement? Dare we believe that He is looking forward to His second coming more than we are?

Needless to say, everyone was deeply touched by that bridegroom's unabated love for his bride. What stirs me even more is to realize this is the way Jesus loves us, His Beloved! The more I read and reflect on Revelation, the more I realize I am just beginning to perceive the intense and involved love of Jesus for His church.

Here Comes the Bride!

In Revelation 2 and 3 the resurrected Jesus addresses His bride, the church, as she currently exists in Asia Minor. The seven churches were all located within a ninety-mile radius of one another, the average distance between them being from twenty-five to fifty miles. They are listed in the text in the order that a carrier going from John's home-in-exile would deliver a circular letter—beginning at Ephesus, which was approximately sixty miles across the Aegean Sea from the Isle of Patmos, and ending in Laodicea.

This is our first of several encounters with the richly symbolic number *seven* in Revelation. We know that there were established churches in at least ten cities in Asia Minor. Why were these seven chosen? Perhaps to give us a composite or full picture of what the bride of Jesus should look like as she "makes herself ready" for the coming of the Bridegroom. We are still praying that the Lord Jesus will transform us into this kind of a church family, right here in Franklin, Tennessee. This is His design, His delight, for His people everywhere.

Each of the seven letters follows a similar form and pattern in construction:

- Jesus addresses the particular church through her resident "angel," either the main leader in the local congregation, a presbyter or bishop, or else a "spiritual guardian angel of that church."

- Jesus is identified by one of the names or images found in John's first vision in Revelation 1:12–18.
- Jesus reveals His intimate knowledge of the church and offers encouragement and commendation, as warranted.
- Rebuke and correction come next as needed. Jesus said, "Those whom I love I rebuke and discipline." (3:19)
- Jesus suggests specific repentance.
- A general exhortation and invitation follows. "He who has an ear, let him hear." (3:22)
- Lastly, Jesus promises a reward (described in terms of the titles and images found in the last two chapters of Revelation).

As we consider each of the seven churches, pay special attention to what our Lord commends and laments about these fellowships. I will paraphrase the overall message to that particular church in the heading.

To the Church in Ephesus: Revelation 2:1–7

Love Me and those around you as you did at first,
with passion and joy.

Ephesus, capital of the Roman province of Asia, teemed with a population of a quarter million citizens. Known as the "Vanity Fair of the Ancient World," she was a wealthy and cosmopolitan trade city, enhanced by sea ports and the convergence of three main highways. Ephesus was also a center of the worship of Artemis, the fertility bee goddess (known by her Latin name Diana in Acts 19). The great temple honoring her in this city became one of the seven wonders of the ancient world.

At the time of John's writing, the church in Ephesus was about thirty years old. The apostle Paul had invested three years of his life preaching the gospel and planting churches there and concluded his great Ephesian epistle with the bene-diction, "Grace to all who love our Lord Jesus Christ with an undying love" (Eph. 6:24). Unfortunately this undying love gave way to "forsaken love." Here is a church commended for her hard work, perseverance, and defense of the faith in the face of heresy. And yet, here is a church which has lost the heart of a bride. She is no longer in love. She is Martha, so busy *for* Jesus, rather than Mary who treasured commu-nion *with* Jesus more than anything else.

The correction that Jesus brings to the Ephesian church is as much a compliment as a rebuke! Do we realize what it means for our Lord to be zealous and jealous for our love? What dignity! What delight! He who loves us with an ever-lasting love is calling for affection and pronounced love, from us, His bride.

As we studied these words in the summer of 1986, we all became convinced and convicted that God's love must be the distinguishing mark of our new church family. We made a covenant to cultivate a Christ-centered worship, one that would enable us to fully express our love and gratitude for our Lord. Our worship services must reflect that we are the well-loved bride of Jesus, a people whose greatest joy is in responding to the affection of our Bridegroom. Empty ritual and predictable liturgy will never do!

We also committed to work hard at expressing the love of Jesus to one another by making forgiveness a predominant theme in our fellowship. As we are loved, so we are to love. Our first leadership family earnestly began praying that God would always grant us community defined by the grace of

God. Many of us in Christ Community come from previous church experiences that are known more by rules and legalism than by healthy relationships and the gospel. We want the word "Community" in our church family's name to be indicative of the mercy and compassion that Jesus has for us. We are convinced that this love will be our most powerful form of evangelism in our culture and the clearest proof that we actually know the Lord. Without love, we are nothing (1 Cor. 13:8).

John was well-acquainted with Jesus' emphasis on love. As he received these words for believers in Ephesus, he remembered the time when our Lord restored Peter to the fellowship of the disciples with this threefold question, "Simon son of John, do you truly love me?" (John 21:15 ff). To have witnessed the intensity of Jesus' compassion as He affirmed the one who had denied Him must have been one of the greatest expressions of love ever seen! To have heard Jesus' emphasis on His longing for our affection no doubt made an indelible impression on John as well. And certainly, he recalled our Lord's summation of the Law and Prophets, when Jesus said, "'Love the Lord your God with all your heart and with all your soul and with all your mind.' This is the first and greatest commandment" (Matt. 22:37–38).

John himself was given the privilege of recording for us the "New Commandment" that Jesus gave His disciples on the evening of His betrayal. "A new command I give you: Love one another. As I have loved you, so you must love one another. By this all men will know that you are my disciples, if you love one another" (John 13:34–35). Love for our Bridegroom must always be our highest priority, and love for one another will be one of the purest and surest demonstrations of this love. It is also John who reminds us, "We love because he first loved us" (1 John 4:19).

To the Church in Smyrna: Revelation 2:8–11

You have suffered much for me, you will suffer more.
Fear not, for I am in control, and I love you.

Smyrna, or Izmir in modern-day Turkey, was about thirty-five miles due north of Ephesus. This proud people minted their own coins, which bore the phrase "First in Asia in beauty and size." Known as a "politically correct" city, Smyrna had a long history of emperor worship. In 195 B.C. the citizens built a temple to Dea Roma, the goddess of Rome, and in A.D. 23 Rome chose this city, above ten other Roman cities, for the sight of a temple to honor Emperor Tiberius. Later, during Domitian's reign (A.D. 81-96), emperor worship became compulsory, and once a year citizens were required to burn incense on the altar to the godhead of Caesar—or face the threat of death.

One can easily imagine that Christians in Smyrna lived under intense pressure to conform to this decree. Rome, however, was not the only source of suffering for the bride. A group of Jews in Smyrna was so hostile to the Christian faith that Jesus refers to them as "a synagogue of Satan." Together they orchestrated a symphony of evil for Jesus' beloved: poverty, slander, prison, and death. This church's love for Jesus was refined in the fire of suffering.

As I read Jesus' letter to Smyrna I am struck by His tenderness, His compassion, and His involved love. To the bride who is suffering He reveals Himself as "the First and the Last, who died and came to life again." Our Bridegroom is eternal and He is victorious! We need not fear death, even death by martyrdom. Jesus has come to "free those who all their lives were held in slavery by their fear of death" (Heb. 2:15).

One of the early church's best-known martyrs was Polycarp, a native of Smyrna. He was put to death in A.D. 156

because of his unwillingness to sacrifice to the emperor: "Eighty and six years have I served Him [Jesus]," Polycarp said, "and He has done me no wrong; how then can I blaspheme my King who saved me?" Few of us realize that there have been more martyrs in the twentieth-century church than in the preceding nineteen centuries combined!

I am also deeply encouraged by the fact that Jesus both acknowledges our suffering and reveals Himself to be the Lord over our pain. "I know your afflictions and your poverty . . . I know the slander" (2:9). Our Bridegroom does not disregard or play down the reality of our hurts. He is no Pollyanna. He who has been made "perfect through suffering" is not "unable to sympathize with our weaknesses" (Heb. 2:10; 4:15).

"Do not be afraid of what you are about to suffer . . . you will suffer persecution for ten days" (2:10). The "ten-day-ness" of this statement is a source of deep comfort. Our Bridegroom, not the devil, is in control of the season of our suffering! He knows our limits, even as He knows His purposes for our sufferings. And He promises that one day we will fully understand the things that are now the source of great fear, hurt, confusion, and even anger. Every tear will be wiped away and all pain redeemed. Therefore, we can learn to say with Paul, "I consider that our present sufferings are not worth comparing with the glory that will be revealed in us" (Rom. 8:18).

The call to suffer actually came as a healing balm to those of us seeking vision for our new church. It has taken years for many of us to recover from the destructive teaching we received in the '60s and '70s which insisted that people of faith will not suffer privation or harm, in any form. How freeing it was (and continues to be) to know that pain and faithfulness go hand in hand. Suffering is actually a sign of the depth of our love, not the lack of our faith.

As a church family we continue to pray that God will enable us to rejoice in our sufferings, to see in the sufferings of our Lord not just the payment for our freedom but also the pattern for our lifestyle. We often ponder as a family of believers, "What will it mean for us to be so captured by the grace and glory of Christ that we, too, will not 'love our lives unto death'"?

To the Church in Pergamum: Revelation 2:12–17

You have loved Me to the point of death and have been
faithful to defend the gospel. I call you, now,
to even greater faithfulness.

Pergamum was located approximately fifty miles up the coast from Smyrna and about ten miles inland. It was a "city set on a hill," in fact on top of a one-thousand-foot hill! Our word *parchment* is derived from *Pergamum*, and for good reasons. Not only was this writing material invented here but the city was also famous for its library of two hundred thousand volumes.

Pergamum was a very religious city with temples and altars to four major pagan cults: Zeus (upon whose huge elevated altar animal sacrifices were offered twenty-four hours a day), Athena (the patron goddess), Dionysos, and Asklepios (the savior gods of healing). Pergamum was also the official Asian center for the imperial cult and the first city with a temple built to honor a living emperor (Augustus in 29 B.C.).

With all of the philosophy and religion in Pergamum it is not hard to understand why this was a persecuted church. Christians commit to a monogamous relationship with the lover of our souls. Jesus tells us, "I am the way and the truth and the life. No one comes to the Father except through me."

This truth is offensive to a world that champions "many ways to the same god." The "sharp, double-edged sword" of the gospel cuts at the heart of a pluralistic culture that esteems religious tolerance over absolute truth. Antipas, a member of the Pergamum church who lost his life for the sake of "true truth," had felt that sword.

If Satan is not successful in destroying the message of the gospel from without, then he will resort to perverting and subverting the gospel from within the church. Jesus rebukes His bride for being inconsistent in her very strength, her love for the truth. Apparently, two strains of false teaching were beginning to infiltrate the church here: the "Baalamites" and the "Nicolaitans." They were compromising with pagan idolatry and immorality, perhaps because they thought Christians were being a little too narrow-minded and a little too legalistic (as some do now). Unfortunately the majority were too nonchalant about this minority. Jesus reminds us, however, that we must not tolerate error under the guise of being open-minded and fair. We can be gracious but still be tenacious for the truth.

I remember with embarrassment one of the first things I uttered after I became a Christian in 1968: "Don't give me theology, give me Jesus!" My assumption was that theology was essentially the same thing as dead orthodoxy. "People who go to seminary are really going to the cemetery," I mused with the shallowness of all such clichés. Little did I realize that every time we say the name "Jesus" we are doing theology! Which Jesus are we talking about when we name His name? The Jesus of the Bible, or of the New Age Movement, or of "prosperity theology," or of Mormonism, or of political liberation movements? They are not the same!

But as my friend Tim Keller, pastor of Redeemer Presbyterian Church in Manhattan, has wisely said, "Live heterodoxy is no answer for dead orthodoxy!" By this he means we must not think the antidote for dead churches full of dry theology is to build "live" churches full of bad theology or even no theology. One of the most loving and vital commitments we can make is to know and to protect the truth of the gospel.

From our study of Jesus' rebuke to the church of Pergamum, our first leadership family in Christ Community formulated the goal of having inflamed hearts based on informed minds. Our pastors, elders, and deacons affirmed early on that no church can afford to be lax about guarding the content of the gospel any more than they can be lax about whom they put into positions of teaching and leadership. Thus, we spend a lot of time and energy teaching and training our leadership family. We want to be a fellowship that gives evidence to live orthodoxy.

George Barna recently presented statistics that demonstrate that while over 80 percent of American evangelicals still profess belief in the inerrancy of the Bible, over 50 percent of them also believe that "absolute truth does not exist."[1] Go figure! Maybe we are in need of a "back to truth movement" so we can have a real "back to the Bible movement."

To the Church in Thyatira: Revelation 2:18–29

Your love for Me is demonstrated in many ways.
Now set your heart on being My holy bride.

Thyatira was forty-five miles southeast of Pergamum on the way to Sardis. Of the seven cities, it was the least in political, religious, and cultural importance. The city was mainly known for its numerous "trade guilds": woolworkers, linenworkers, makers of outer garments, dyers, leatherworkers, tanners, potters, bakers, slave dealers, and bronzesmiths (a union town if I ever saw one!). Lydia, a seller of purple goods and the apostle Paul's first convert to Christianity in Macedonia, was from Thyatira (Acts 16:14 ff).

The One who sees everything, with His "eyes of blazing fire," looks into the heart of the church there and finds much to affirm. This bride has made steady progress in her "deeds, love, faith, service, and perseverance." She is quite the picture of health and maturity. What more could Jesus long for?

Yet the trade guilds were so integrated into the religious life of the community, that economics and worship practices went hand-in-hand. In order to be licensed to do business in the community, local merchants had to belong to one of the many guilds, each of which was tied to the worship of a particular god. Apparently the economic pressure of buying and selling in an economy in which business was tied to false worship was taking its toll on a part of the church. Many Christians were succumbing to the pressure to compromise their faith in order to provide financially for their families.

This economic pressure led to moral compromise. As John Stott says, "If the devil cannot conquer the church by the application of political pressure or the propagation of intellectual heresy he will try by the insinuation of moral evil."[2]

Another deadly source of moral compromise among the believers in Thyatira was a certain "Jezebel." She, like her Old Testament counterpart, represents either an individual or group which had infiltrated the church with the power of seduction. Apparently some of the believers of the church in Thyatira were being led into idolatry and immorality through the false teaching of this "Jezebel party." It would appear that the theology of the church was being reshaped by this "prophetess." I see her as an early representation of what Dietrich Bonhoeffer would later refer to as "cheap grace." By retooling the gospel to fit the economic and moral climate of the culture, Christians in Thyatira were led to believe that "grace" frees us to fit into any society without challenging its values and mores. How foolish and naive these believers were!

In confronting this evil, Jesus calls His bride to a more consistent and consuming holiness.

Holiness is one of those concepts that has fallen on hard times in the contemporary church. Before I became a Christian I saw this word as synonymous with dourness, dowdiness, religious rules, the interjection "NO!", and mean-spirited people, who did anything but make the gospel attractive to me. But as God has given me grace, I realize that holiness is an attitude of the heart, even before it is compliance with a list of "do's and don'ts." To be "holy" is simply to be "set apart" for God's purposes.

We who have been declared holy through the gospel by justification are being made progressively holy by sanctification, as God conforms us more and more unto the image of Jesus. And thanks be to God! He promises to bring to completion the good work He has begun in us (Phil. 1:6).

Holiness is also our radical commitment to live out the implications of what it means to be the tenderly loved bride of Jesus. We are to live for the pleasure and praise of Jesus, not that He might accept us, but because we are thankful that He already has—fully and eternally! Any other motivation turns our obedience into legalism and self-righteousness.

Naïveté and compromise must be rejected. We must guard against being absorbed into our culture for the sake of economic or social benefit. But let us also guard against confusing holiness with moralism, which leads to asceticism, withdrawal, or alienation from our culture. Neither laxity nor legalism is the answer. We are to be "in the world and yet not of it." We are to demonstrate to the "watching world" what it means to be captured by the love of Jesus. As a betrothed bride, let us keep ourselves pure and holy for our true love.

Our church family continues to wrestle with the call to a love-motivated holiness that we embraced our first year. It is so easy to fall back into a performance-based spirituality, into the ugliness of self-righteousness and mere moralism. But it is just as easy to misuse our freedom in Christ, to wrongly assume that God's grace makes us less responsible to live lives that are pleasing to Him. We are beginning to realize that grace actually frees us and empowers us to obey God. Thus, we are discovering the beauty of holiness.

To the Church in Sardis: Revelation 3:1–6

My heart breaks when I think of you, for you are in name only, My Bride. I call you to life; I call you to reality.

Sardis was located about thirty miles south of Thyatira, and, in the sixth century B.C., was one of the most powerful cities of the ancient world, marked by times of commercial and military notoriety. Three main landmarks were prominent:

- the acropolis, which rose eight hundred feet above the north section of Sardis;
- the temple to Artemis; and
- the necropolis, or cemetery, of "a thousand hills," burial mounds which could be seen on the skyline seven miles from the city.

King Croesus lived here with all of his pomp and wealth. Through negligence and a lack of vigilance, however, Sardis was attacked and defeated several times. An earthquake also devastated the city in A.D. 17, and only through the generosity of Emperor Tiberius was Sardis able to recover and become a successful center for the wool and dye industry. As a city, it had been known for "luxury and laxity" and came to represent "the peace of the man whose dreams are dead

and whose mind is asleep, the peace of lethargy and eva-
sion."³

No other church incurs a more severe rebuke from Jesus
than Sardis. Here is an example of a bride in name only. Her
reputation was without reality, her creed without Christ, her
religion without relationship. The church in Sardis became
"a perfect model of inoffensive Christianity,"⁴ the first example of nominal Christianity in the New Testament.

The One "who holds the seven spirits" (John's description
of the Holy Spirit in Revelation) confronts this deadness. The
bride of Jesus is not to be a lifeless mannequin in the window
of the religious marketplace or a fading image in the scrap-
book of ecclesiastical memory. We are called to life in the
Spirit, which is generated and sustained by Jesus Himself.

Is it possible for entire congregations to be "in church"
but not "in Christ"? Jesus' very sobering words, "You have
a reputation of being alive, but you are dead" (3:1), seem
to answer in the affirmative. But how does a church fall into
such a lamentable condition?

As a young Christian in the "Jesus Movement," I used to
think this rebuke was addressed primarily to individual
Christians who simply needed to be revived! Although an
appropriate application of the letter to Sardis, I now realize,
after having been a pastor for nearly twenty years, that religious and social enculturation can be so strong and deceptive
that large groups of professing Christians can go through the
motions of religious life and neither understand the gospel
nor experience its saving power. Jesus warns us, in the Sermon on the Mount, that many will come on the day of judgment assuming membership in His kingdom based on
participation in spiritual activity or even supernatural manifestations of God's Spirit. But He will say to them, "I never
knew you: depart from me," (Matt. 7:23, KJV).

Jesus recognized that there were some genuine Christians

in Sardis, however (as there are in most dead churches), who "walk with me, dressed in white" (3:4). These are not an example of "the deeper-life club" or a "spiritual elite" in the church. Rather, they alone are the bride. I assumed (perhaps as other Christians have) that I was a Christian until the very night I was converted. We dare not equate being in the pews with being in Christ!

Our study of the church in Sardis was very sobering. We began petitioning God in those first months to keep us from ever confusing mere enthusiasm with real life in the Spirit. Our goal became not just to ignite the religious flesh, something that can be easily done by simply "pushing the right spiritual buttons." Rather, our longing was expressed in terms of becoming a church in which the real presence of the Lord would be known. We passionately wanted to be a fellowship in which men and women could have a genuine encounter with the living God.

We also realized the importance of continuing to preach the gospel within the church and to never be presumptuous about who is and who is not in Christ. In a southern culture like ours, there are so many individuals who come to church for years without ever coming to Christ. It has been our joy to see members of churches become members of the Body of Christ.

To the Church in Philadelphia: Revelation 3:7–13

I write you only to encourage you and to strengthen your hearts. You are placed in a key position to impact your culture and the nations. Trust Me. I am using you for my glory.

Philadelphia, situated thirty-five miles southeast of Sardis, was located at the eastern end of a broad valley near the river Cogamis. The city was at the juncture of trade routes leading to Mysia, Lydia, and Phrygia, earning Philadelphia the title, "gateway to the East." Her economic prowess was based on agriculture and industry. Strabo, the historian, called Philadelphia "a city full of earthquakes." The great earthquake of A.D. 17 hit Sardis but nearly destroyed Philadelphia. But by the time of John's writing, the city, which had been rebuilt and was known as "little Athens," was brimming with temples and religious festivals. The persecution that Christians experienced did not come from the pagans, however, it came primarily from hostile Jews.

Jesus reveals Himself to the beloved of Philadelphia as the Lord of opportunity. He has the "key of David," which controls the opening and closing of all doors. "What he opens no one can shut, and what he shuts no one can open" (3:7). In this church we find a thrilling example of strength in weakness. This small, seemingly insignificant body of believers is called to go through a great door of opportunity into a life of substantive impact. What a paradox!

The gospel is full of such glorious paradoxes. (In fact, this is one of Mike Card's favorite themes.) The way to live is to die. The first shall be last. The way up is down. We find ourselves by losing ourselves. As Paul wrote, "We have this treasure in jars of clay to show that this all-surpassing power is from God and not from us" (2 Cor. 4:7).

As I read Jesus' words to His bride in Philadelphia, I am both encouraged and rebuked. First of all, I am encouraged that He is the One through whom and by whom all ministry is realized. Jesus calls us, gifts us, and empowers us to be involved in His eternal purposes. The Great Commission, for example, is not a "job to get done" but rather a reality in which we participate. We need to see ministry as the overflow of hearts filled with the grace of the gospel. Jesus uses His people to do things they cannot do in their own power. "God chose the foolish things of the world to shame the wise; God chose the weak things of the world to shame the strong. He chose the lowly things of this world and the despised things—and the things that are not—to nullify the things that are" (1 Cor. 1:27–28). The church in Philadelphia was to see itself like Gideon's army, a little people with a big and faithful God.

This letter also rebukes me, and perhaps many of us in the contemporary "fortress church." Believers in Philadelphia were placed in a strategic location in a pagan culture. All they had to do was walk through the door of opportunity and ministry. Their calling was not to build "Camp God" and be a community of ingrown navel-gazers merely holding on "till the rapture." Their calling, and ours, is to be "salt and light." We are not merely to selfishly fill up our "Day-timers" with endless "fellowship" opportunities with other Christians.

This is our Father's world! Non-Christians are not our ultimate enemy, Satan is. Why does such a strident "us versus them" dichotomy persist? We are to build bridges, not burn them.

Ministry can get very messy, exhausting, and painful. Persecution is the predictable consequence of a commitment to witness faithfully. But Jesus promises, "I will make them [those who persecute us] come and fall down at your feet and acknowledge that I have loved you" (3:9). What an image! What a promise! Ministry is following our Lord through any and every door that He opens.

As we reflected upon Jesus' letter to Philadelphia we drew three conclusions for our new church family: First, we promised not to become a busy, program-driven church. There are some churches that keep their members so preoccupied with meetings and programs that they have precious little time to have relationships with non-Christians. We want all of our members to be in relationship with those in our culture who, like us, desperately need the grace of God.

Second, we embraced the call to extend the "welcoming heart of God" through all of the ministries of our church. We have not always been faithful to this calling, but our Lord has been most gracious in giving us an atmosphere in which many non-Christians have expressed their feeling of acceptance and love as they begin their spiritual quests in our midst.

Third, we committed to "outgrow" Christ Community Church. That is, by embracing and keeping a high emphasis on world evangelization, we will guard against becoming an ingrown fellowship, simply preoccupied with ourselves.

The bottom line is this: Jesus is the "friend of sinners." Are we?

To the Church in Laodicea: Revelation 3:14–22

Wake up my bride! Your heart has become tepid, divided, and proud. I call you to Myself.

Laodicea, situated in the Lycus valley near the cities of Hierapolis and Colossae, about forty miles southeast of Philadelphia, was considered the chief city of the southern region of Phrygia. A very wealthy town, it was known for its banking industry and its medical school, which produced "Phrygian powder," a popular eye salve. After being severely debilitated by an earthquake in A.D. 61, the city refused financial assistance from Rome, choosing to rebuild from her own treasury.

Ranchers there raised a prized species of sheep whose black, glossy wool was in great demand. The city's major weakness was its lack of a convenient source of water; city planners had built the city because of trade routes, not because of its natural resources.

Here we have a picture of an immature, spoiled bride who is blind to her own condition. Jesus confronts His beloved with her spiritual self-satisfaction, complacency, and indifference.

John Stott says of this church, "Perhaps none of the seven letters is more appropriate to the 20th century church than this. It describes vividly the respectable, sentimental, nominal, skin-deep religiosity which is so widespread today. Our Christianity is flabby and anemic. We appear to have taken a lukewarm bath of religion. Zeal, heat, fire, passion—these are the qualities we lack today and desperately need."[5]

Jesus' rebuke to the Laodiceans manifests the depth of His compassion and concern for His people, for "those whom I love I rebuke and discipline" (3:19). "Faithful are the wounds of a friend," Proverbs tells us, and this Friend is Jesus.

Laodicea is an example of a church (or a Christian) that fails to realize the power the "good life" has to dilute our wholehearted affection for Jesus. Michael Card told me of a visit he had with a couple of national pastors who had been imprisoned for nearly twenty years by communist revolutionaries for no other reason than that they preached the gospel. He recounted their commitment "to pray about the poverty of the wealth of the American church." Riches and comforts, they feared, were too much of a burden for Christians to carry. "How can we be free to love and to worship and to serve Jesus when weighed down with the things of this world?" they lovingly asked. Ouch!

Hear the cry of the Lover of our souls as He calls out to us, "Here I am! I stand at the door and knock. If anyone hears my voice and opens the door, I will come in and eat with him, and he with me" (3:20). This is not an evangelistic appeal to non-Christians. It is Jesus' appeal to His bride to realize the tragedy of worldly comforts replacing communion with Him. He longs for the rich fellowship of the table; and every time we partake of the Lord's Supper we should long for the day when we will eat with him at the "wedding supper of the Lamb" (Rev. 19:9).

Since the first time we partook of the Lord's Supper as a new church ten years ago, this blessed sacrament has stirred within us deep longings for this Day. We don't just look back to the cross, we look ahead to the crown, and our hearts are richly blessed!

As our group studied these seven letters, we took notice of the type of bride for which Jesus longs. This became the objective for our new church, and the personal standard for each one of us.

The Bride Beautiful

1. A passionate "first love" relationship with the Lord Jesus that spills over into all other relationships;
2. A willingness to suffer for our Bridegroom;
3. A growing knowledge of the truth of the gospel and a commitment to defend the faith "once and for all delivered unto the saints";
4. A purity of heart and holiness of lifestyle, driven by love and empowered by grace;
5. An aliveness in Jesus generated by His real presence in our midst and hearts;
6. A commitment to follow Jesus into a life of other-centered living through evangelism, missions, and cultural impact;
7. An undivided and wholehearted allegiance to Jesus, which treasures communion with Him more than the comforts of the world—more than anything else.

How we, the contemporary American church, need to ponder these things in the waning moments of the twentieth century! I was present at a lecture in the '70s where theologian

Francis Schaeffer warned us of his fear that we were headed for a day when the consuming preoccupation of American evangelicals would be only for "personal peace and affluence."

I believe that the self-absorbing narcissism of our culture has given birth to "McChurch," a generation of consumer-driven churches competing with each other like fast-food restaurants. Something is tragically wrong when a prominent church leader in our day will suggest that the only reformation we need is one of "self-affirmation." God have mercy on us! No matter what our denomination, theological heritage, or liturgical preference, we need revival in the American church!

TO THE OVERCOMERS

To him who overcomes, I will give . . .

FROM THE SONG

The promises given to those whom Jesus confidently calls "overcomers" are consistently repeated throughout the seven letters to the churches. Each time, a unique promise is given: "To the one who overcomes . . .

- I will give the right to eat from the tree of life, which is the paradise of God (2:7).
- [They] will not be hurt at all by the second death (2:11).
- I will give some of the hidden manna. I will also give him a white stone with a new name written on it, known only to him who receives it (2:17).
- I will give authority over the nations (2:26).

- I will also give him the morning star (2:28).
- [They will] be dressed in white (3:5).
- I will make a pillar in the temple of my God (3:12).
- I will give the right to sit with me on my throne" (3:21).

The overcomers are promised unique rewards because they themselves are unique men and women. They have used their imaginations, their hearts, and their minds to withstand persecution and temptation—and everything else that the evil one has hurled at them. Despite the desperate situation of their time, they have lived their lives convinced of the reality of unseen things. By grace, they have overcome it all.

Even as these promises rang in those first-century ears, so they are meant to echo in ours as well. For we are to become overcomers. And we are to accomplish this victory precisely as our sisters and brothers two thousand years ago accomplished it: by faith in Him who makes and keeps all His promises.

Along with our ancient brothers we should be warned, as well, that not everyone John is writing to will be an overcomer. Many will compromise the faith; many will listen to false teaching; many will give in to fear. Apostasy is a reality.

Yet Jesus speaks words of comfort—as well as words of warning—to those who might be faltering. Again and again He says, "I know . . ."

- "I know your deeds, your hard work" (2:2).
- "I know that you cannot tolerate wicked men" (2:2).
- "I know your afflictions and your poverty" (2:9).
- "I know where you live" (2:13).
- "I know your deeds, your love and faith, your service and perseverance" (2:19).

Jesus reveals Himself as the One who "searches hearts and minds." He knows their sufferings and weaknesses since He has experienced the same temptations and weaknesses. For it is Jesus Himself who is the ultimate Overcomer in the book of Revelation.

And so the Overcomer speaks to comfort those who will become overcomers. The Promised One promises to give them hope, to give them Himself, and to ultimately make them like Himself.

To the Overcomers

I know your deeds. I've seen your service.
I recognize the reputation of your lives.
But I know you live near Satan's shadow,
And I've seen your faithful struggle to survive.

And to the one who overcomes
I'll give the manna.
He'll have a pure white stone
With his own secret name.
She will possess the morning star in all its splendor—
All this and more for them because they overcame.

So just hold on, do not grow weary.
For I am He who searches hearts and minds.
Behold I'm standing at the door,
And I am knocking.
And the one who hears and opens it will find (that)

The one who overcomes will rule the nations.
On the throne he'll sit beside me dressed in white.
She will become a column in God's holy Temple.
They all will eat freely from the tree of Life.

The overcomers come to understand
That they are precious poems printed
In the palms of His hands.

CHAPTER THREE

REVELATION 4
THE HOPE
OF AN OCCUPIED THRONE

FROM THE WORD

A couple of summers ago I took my wife and two kids to Western Europe to visit some of the missionaries our church family is privileged to support. We traveled through France, Italy, and Switzerland before ending up in England. That one trip generated enough stories of "rapture and rupture" to justify a book all to itself. Before you plan any "exciting and romantic" overnight train voyages on Eurail, get in touch with me! Talk about making family memories. Why did the summer of 1994 have to be the hottest in a hundred years in those wonderful European countries? I really sound like missionary material, don't I?

All things considered, it really was a great trip, and certainly one of the most enjoyable highlights of the whole expedition was the city of London. While visiting with our missionaries who are seeking to love and preach the gospel among the huge Asian and Indian population, we were fortunate to be able to visit many of the historic landmarks of that great English capital. One such foray into the annals of the important found me and my two kids, Kristin and Scott, indulging ourselves with the "Beatle-walk," a walking tour

of many of the London-based highlights in the history of the
The Beatles.

As fun as that was, my favorite "typical tourist" experience actually took place not on Abbey Road but in Westminster Abbey. I am not sure what I was expecting to find on
the inside of this majestic Anglican cathedral as I waited in
line, or as the English say, "in queue." Overwhelmed is an
overused word, but that's what it felt like as I walked into
what seemed more like a museum in honor of the dead than
a house of worship for the living. Poets, musicians, states-
men, politicians, all kinds of great people from Great Britain
are remembered by plaques, parquets, or by sarcophagi.
(There goes the alliteration!)

As we made our way toward the back of the stately and
crowded cathedral I had no idea what I was going to find
placed directly behind the chancel area. Strategically located
and welcoming every visitor's touch was the coronation
throne used for kings since the twelfth century! Suddenly I
was very aware of just how young America is. We're toddlers
in a world of grown-ups. Men and women of renown who
influenced the course of history sat upon this ancient piece of
furniture which gave new meaning to the word "antique."

Close by were the remains of several of the kings and
queens who have graced, and sometimes disgraced, the history of the English commonwealth. That moment quickened
within me an understanding and appreciation of the biblical
themes of "kingship" and "kingdom" I previously embraced
only in theological or theoretical categories.

John's readers most definitely thought in terms of kings
and crowns and thrones. These royal tokens represented life
and death to the citizens dwelling in the Roman world.
Christians first tasted the political insanity of Emperor Nero
as he sought to blame the burning of Rome on this ragtag
bunch of religious fanatics who worshiped a dead man. He

was even known occasionally to dip believers in pitch and light them as lamps at his parties. And let's remember, as John writes from Patmos, Emperor Domitian is on the throne and he is demanding to be addressed as "lord and god." Under his reign, those who call Jesus Lord and God are being severely persecuted and put to death. The Roman "throne" was a source of fear and anxiety for John's readers and a means of unparalleled suffering. What, then, will Jesus want His Church, His Bride—as represented by the seven churches—to see and know?

How profoundly comforting it is to meditate upon the significance of the next vision that Jesus reveals to John against this political backdrop. Revelation 4 begins with the image of a door "standing open in heaven" (4:1). No doubt this door was opened from the heavenward side. The same Lord who opens a door of opportunity for believers in Philadelphia (3:8) now opens a door for John (and us!) that allows a glimpse into heaven. The trumpet-like voice of authority which the apostle has already heard continues with an invitation to "come up here." Our Lord loves to reveal Himself! John is promised insight into "what *must* take place . . ." Here is that awesome word *must* appearing once again in the text. God's will *is* going to be accomplished on earth, even as it is in heaven! We have His promise. John provides us with a graphic basis for our assurance as Jesus now shows him what is going on behind the scenes, right now.

Through the person of the Holy Spirit, John is given a vision of heaven, with all of its glorious persona and perfection. It is of mammoth significance that we notice the very first thing upon which his gaze is fixed as the panorama of eternity is presented. Amid all of the sights, sounds, and plethora of symbols, images, and beings, that which captures John's attention and focus is "a throne in heaven with someone sitting on it" (4:2). This symbol of power and authority occurs forty times in the text of Revelation. However, he doesn't just see a throne, but an *occupied* throne. God is in session! The *real* throne is in heaven, not in Rome. God rules, not Domitian! In the light of this throne, and the dominion of the One sitting upon it, all other claims to kingly rule become vain and empty. All of the kings of the earth are like the Wizard of Oz, little men who make a lot of noise behind big curtains.

What makes this throne magnificent is not the grain of the wood, a finely detailed carving, or a jewel-encrusted headboard. In fact, John does not describe the royal chair at all. Just the One who occupies this seat of sovereignty, He alone is central to the whole of eternity and time. Consistent with Jewish tradition, John does not attempt to tell us what God looks like, for fear of even the slightest misrepresentation. All he can say of God is that He "had the appearance of jasper and carnelian" (4:3). These two precious or semiprecious stones probably represent God's brilliance and majesty. Our God is altogether glorious.

Around the throne was "a rainbow, resembling an emerald" (4:3). The rainbow has special meaning in the history of redemption since the moment God promised Noah that He would never again destroy the world by water (Gen. 9:15–17). To see a rainbow in the sky is to be reminded, therefore, of God's mercy and covenantal faithfulness. But the rainbow which John sees in heaven has even more glorious features. First of all, it "encircled the throne" (4:3). This is not the typical half-circle that we are used to seeing after it rains. It is a complete circle, perhaps indicating the all-encompassing mercies of God in everything He does. The mono-chromatic emerald color of this rainbow conveys the multidimensional peace of lush, green "meadows and distant forests."

Underneath such a canopy of glory and around the throne

John counts "twenty-four other thrones, and seated on them were twenty-four elders. They were dressed in white and had crowns of gold on their heads" (4:4). This is the first of many circles of beings emanating from the throne. The significance of the placement of God's enthronement in John's vision should be obvious. All things center on Him! All things are concentric to Him.

Who, then, are these twenty-four elders? Probably, they represent the totality of redeemed mankind from both the Old and New Covenant communities, symbolized by the twelve patriarchs of Israel and the twelve apostles of Jesus. In keeping with this interpretation their white garments represent the imputed righteousness of the Lord Jesus, given to all who receive the grace of God in the gospel (Rev. 3:4 ff, 18; 7:9; 19:8, 14). The gold crowns signify both our calling to reign with Him as a kingdom of priests and the rewards for faithful service that Jesus promises to His people (Rev. 3:21; 22:5). What an encouraging picture is painted for us: The whole people of God represented by our faithful leaders in perfect relationship to God and to one another.

Please do not think of heaven as having the controlled and muted climate of a library! "From the throne came flashes of lightning, rumblings and peals of thunder" (4:5). Should this remind us of Mt. Sinai and other times when God spoke and acted in nature? (Ex. 19:16; Ps. 18:13–15; 1 Sam. 2:10). The third member of the Trinity, the Holy Spirit ("the seven spirits" of God, cf. Rev. 1:4), is presented in close proximity to the throne in all of His fullness and fiery presence (Matt. 3:11; Acts 2:3 ff; 1 Pet. 1:7; 1 Cor. 3:12 ff). He is so faithful to accomplish the purposes of God the Father with blazing effectiveness throughout the universe and in all of history.

How inviting it is for John next to see and describe "what looked like a sea of glass, clear as crystal" (4:6). This immense and serene body of water before our enthroned heavenly Father conveys the presence of a peace that passes all understanding. No troubled waters here, no consternation or doubt. He is never surprised. God loses sleep about nothing. In fact, He never "sleeps nor slumbers." He is not pacing around heaven hoping things are going to work out. Neither is He our glorified cheerleader, merely rooting and pulling for us in the "game of life." He is *our* God, "working all things together after the counsel of his will," and "working in all things for the good of those who love him." We need to lay hold of this glorious truth as much as our brothers and sisters in the first-century church.

As we continue in the text of Revelation we are going to find more complex symbols and images that require suggestive rather than dogmatic interpretation. However, even when we disagree about things inconclusive in the text, many clear and abiding principles can be drawn from these Scriptures without our having absolute confidence about the meaning of each detail. Such is the case with the four eye-encrusted living creatures, who are mentioned fourteen times in Revelation. As we consider the whole of Scriptures, it would seem that this quartet is meant to represent either all of animate creation: the lion is the king of wild beasts, the ox is the king of domesticated beasts, the eagle is the king of the birds of the air, and man is king of animate creation. Or, perhaps, as others have suggested, they represent the angelic order of angels known in the Bible as "cherubim" (Ezek. 10:20; Gen. 3:24; Ex. 25:20). Both Ezekiel and Isaiah describe visions of angels that include six wings (Isa. 6; Ezek. 1).

The number "four" should make us think of the four corners of the earth (Rev. 20:8), the four winds (Rev. 7:1), or the four compass points (Luke 13:29; Ps. 107:3). The multitudinous eyes seem to imply constant vigilance. Both interpretations have in common the reference to creation and God's involvement and watchfulness over all that He has made. "This *is* my Father's world . . .", as the hymn writer has well said. There is no place where He is not Lord. All of creation reflects His glory. In all of creation His angels do His bidding. Be encouraged, small, persecuted church. Be warned, haughty Roman empire. Tremble with fear, Satan and your host of darkness. God is on the throne and He is in the center of all things!

This is not a static, sixteenth-century classic oil painting hanging in the Louvre. This is the dynamic of heaven. These things are going on even as John is "in the Spirit." The four living creatures are, as their name implies, alive! The apostle sees and hears their persistent activity. "Day and night they never stop saying: 'Holy, holy, holy is the Lord God Almighty, who was, and is, and is to come'" (4:8). With this act of praise we begin to understand that worship is the constant disposition of the residents of heaven.

In this first hymn of heaven John reminds us that God is altogether "other" in His essential being. He is "holy." He is absolutely pure even as He is absolutely sovereign. The "trisagion"—"Holy, holy, holy"—is important for us to ponder for this is the only attribute of God that is trebled in the entire Bible. And as God is augustly holy, so He also is praised for His timelessness. He is the One "who was, and is, and is to come" (4:8). He has no boundaries or limitations. Neither does He have any lack or any need. He is complete, within His own Triune existence, thoroughly content and incredibly joyous. Theologians in the past referred to this perfection of God as His "asaiety."

As God is adored by the four living creatures "the twenty-four elders fall down before him who sits on the throne, and worship him who lives for ever and ever" (4:10). This act of prostration is the appropriate and repeated sign of affectionate reverence to the One who alone is "worthy, our Lord and

God" (4:11). Again, let it be known that God, not Domitian or any other earthly ruler, deserves such honor and adoration. As the elders lay down their bodies they also lay down their crowns "before the throne." This symbol of submission is also an acknowledgment that their reign is derivative and their rewards are really tokens of God's operative grace. We will not preen around heaven like proud Boy Scouts with sashes full of merit badges. God will get full glory for everything that He was pleased to accomplish through His people.

The elders proclaim God's worth as they cry out "you created all things, and by your will they were created and have their being" (4:11). The Father is worshiped in this hymn as the origin, source, architect, designer, builder, essence, reason, and end of *all* things. To see Him upon His throne is to be humbled and to be gladdened for our God has no equals or rivals. He will never be threatened, overthrown, or impeached. Who can ultimately resist His will? "Of Him and through Him and to Him are all things." "In Him we live and move and have our being."

The order of John's visions is important. Before the apostle is given a vision of the unfolding of history through the breaking of the seven seals, his eyes and heart must be captured by a sight of the Lord of history. Difficult things do and will happen to the people of God. But who is in control? This knowledge is central and critical to everything that now follows in Revelation and in all of life.

Nothing exists in the past, present, or in the future, apart from God's will. Everything that happens on earth has an inseparable heavenly counterpart and everything in Revelation 6–22 flows out of the throne-room vision in Revelation 4–5.

How desperately our generation of Christians needs a fresh vision and understanding of the sovereignty of God. We are not fatalists. Patty Page is not our patron theological saint as she sang, "Que sera, sera, whatever will be, will be."

Neither are we stoics, who brace ourselves against the storms of life and accept all things with passive resignation. Neither must we allow ourselves to become superficial evangelicals, full of denial about the reality of pain and suffering, groping for one more biblical Band-Aid and spiritual anesthetic to deal with huge and troubling issues which are an inevitable part of the Christian life.

Without this vision of the occupied throne many come to the symbols and images in Revelation—like the Antichrist, the great tribulation, beasts, dragons, Babylon, 666, famines, and wars—and end up feeding their fears rather than their faith. What an utter shame! It angers me when I consider the countless number of Christians who have been deprived of the implications of this great throne-room vision through poor, inadequate, and wrong teaching. Martin Luther was right when he stated that "bad theology is the worst taskmaster of all." God is robbed of the glory due His name and believers are bereft of peace, joy, and hope won for them by Jesus. This should not be the case. It just does not have to be!

There are no accidents or coincidences for the people of God, just God's loving, if sometimes hard to accept, providences. Coming to accept and rejoice in the sovereignty of God has been a lifelong struggle of mine, beginning with the death of my mom in a car wreck when I was only eleven years old. It just made no sense to me that God would leave me motherless just as I was beginning those precarious adolescent years. I lamented it then. I lament it now. But God has, indeed, proven to me that His name is Redeemer. I have to learn this lesson over and over.

Just last year one of the pastors on our staff was brutally murdered. Last month a perfectly healthy forty-five-year-old dad and husband in our church dropped dead. Last week my son was in a car wreck that totaled a Jeep Cherokee and could easily have been fatal for him and for his friend who was driving. And in the last few hours I have received the heart-wrenching news that my mentor and discipler of twenty-one years has been taken to heaven. Dr. Jack Miller, the man who taught me and showed me more of the grace of the gospel than anyone, has gone to the real home. I would never begrudge Jack one day in heaven, but right now my heart breaks. I would never have scripted his death for this day after Easter Sunday.

And yet, how appropriate for Jack to die today, the day after we celebrated the greatest and most loving demonstration of the sovereign mercy and might of the One upon the throne.

Oh, the despair that would fill my soul if I did not believe with every fiber of my being that God loves and that He is in control. Thank God, there is an occupied throne in heaven.

YOU ARE WORTHY

Revelation 4

FROM THE SONG

We read John's amazing visions. We seek to see with the mind's eye what it must have been like to be there. We strain with our ears to hear the silent music of the great songs of warning and praise. And deep inside ourselves, even before the most terrifying of the visions, we long to have been there, and even now to find a way there. And there is a way.

John was transported from the isle of Patmos, away from the choking dust of the quarry to which he had been condemned, literally to another time and another place. In the same manner Isaiah and Daniel had been transported—out of their time and place by the vehicle of vision—as much as eight hundred years before.

For these biblical prophets, this transport into the heavenlies was an experience over which they seemed to have little or no control, apart from their own obedient willingness to be God's men at that time, in that place.

Today, for us, God provides another means by which we cover the distance: the vehicle of worship, which can transport us to that miraculous heavenly place. We, too, can take our place alongside the multitude and sing the same songs. We can, in faith, be present at the very throne of God.

If you are rolling your eyes at this notion and thinking, *"I see no throne when I worship,"* you misunderstand the real purpose of worship. It is not to provide us with an *experience*. Regardless of whether we might be aware of our presence alongside the heavenly multitude, faith tells us we are, in fact, together with them, bonded by worship, giving our praise to Him. Worship, like visionary experience, transcends time and space, for the Object of worship is transcendent. Your shouts and songs and words of worship are heard by the same God in the same throne room, and in precisely the same place—beyond time! Whenever we truly worship, we worship with the saints.

Holy, Holy, Holy

Holy, Holy, Holy
Is the Lord Almighty.
Who was and is
And is to come.

Holy, Holy, Holy
Is the Lord Almighty.
Holy, Holy, Holy
Is the Lord.

You Are Worthy

I wept for none was worthy
To open the scroll
Or to look upon what it contained
Then a voice said, "See the Lion
Of the tribe of Judah."
So I looked to the Lion
And saw a Lamb that was slain.

Worthy is the Lamb
That was slain
To receive power, wealth,
And wisdom and strength
And honor and glory
And praise evermore;
Worthy is the Lamb
That was slain!

From every tribe and language
People and nation
Your blood purchased men for God
You won them a kingdom by your salvation
And made them priests to serve our God.

Worthy is the Lamb
That was slain
To receive power, wealth,
And wisdom and strength
And honor and glory
And praise evermore;

Worthy is the Lamb
That was slain!

You are worthy
To take up
And open the scroll,
For You are the Lamb
That was slain;
Glory and honor
To the One on the throne,
To the Lamb
Who lives and reigns.

CHAPTER FOUR

REVELATION 5:1–8; 11–14
THE HOPE OF THE PERFECTED
WORSHIP OF HEAVEN

FROM THE WORD

It is hard to believe that I have been a Christian for almost three decades. That's over a quarter of a century's worth of learning how much I need the grace of God every single day. During that time I have had the privilege of experiencing, firsthand, the enormity and the diversity of the Body of Christ. Travel, through various missions and ministry opportunities, has been just as important to my theological education and spiritual formation as my seminary training. Both have been needed, but in recent years it seems that my cross-cultural excursions have been critical to the deepening of my repentance from privatizing and Americanizing the gospel. God has all kinds of sons and daughters, through redemption and adoption in Christ, who love Him equally, but who also love Him differently. The body of Christ is the real "rainbow coalition."

Through my travels and from studying church history it has become redundantly obvious to me that we Christians don't tend to handle our rich diversity very well at all. No scandal of the contemporary church is more pronounced than the multiplicity of denominations, which defines the

Christian topography. As our Lord has prayed for our unity, mutual esteem, and love, we have majored on the theological minor, ecclesiastical turf protection, and straining out gnats while swallowing camels. Oh, that this would grieve our hearts the way it must certainly grieve our Lord's!

One who lamented our divided state of affairs wrote this parody of a familiar hymn:

> Like a mighty tortoise
> Moves the Church of God;
> Brothers we are treading
> Where we've always trod;
> We are all divided,
> Many bodies we,
> Very strong on doctrine,
> Weak on charity.

Painfully, and oddly enough, our disunity is nowhere more clearly pronounced than when the topic of "worship" emerges for discussion and planning among Christians. That which is meant to be an expression of Spirit-wrought humility and other-centered adoration of God often becomes a battleground for proud combatants to vie for the right to define the liturgy and control the elements of the worship service. More often than not, this is usually only determined by a person's aesthetic sensibilities and preferences—not theology.

Even in individual church families, I have observed more suspicion, anger, manipulation, and hostility surrounding the control of the worship service than of the predictable "war zones." What an ugly circumstance and utter contradiction of the nature and purpose of the worship of God! How can this be? It should also grieve us that the most segregated and provincial hour of the week occurs on the Lord's Day when we gather to worship the Head of the *whole* Church. Talk about *non sequiturs*! The book of Revelation confronts these sins and invites us to something far more glorious. In Revelation 5, we are still in the great throne room. As we look at this whole section within the apocalypse, it becomes obvious that John is given much more than a vision of the sovereignty of God with his glimpse into the control center of the universe. He is given a vision of the glorious worship of heaven! John sees and hears that for which we have been made, that which will be our sumptuous feast throughout eternity, the perfected worship of our Triune God. As Karl Barth has said, "Christian worship is the most momentous, the most urgent, the most glorious action that can take place in human life."[1] John's visions of heavenly worship bear this out.

From this point on we will see that the worship of the Lamb and the One upon the throne is the defining reality of the people of God. It distinguishes us from those who worship the beast (Rev. 13), demons, and idols. It is the love song of the bride for the Bridegroom. It is the means by which we are to wage war against Satan in the world, not against one another in the body of Christ. It is the eschatological cry of the beloved of the Lord who worship now as a foretaste of how we will worship then.

Worship is presented as a way of life, and not just that which is celebrated one day a week in a special room called the "worship center." The whole of God's creation is the "worship center" and God Himself is the center of all worship. Several hymns and doxologies are intentionally and strategically placed throughout Revelation, leading me to believe that the apocalypse is to the New Testament what the book of Psalms is to the Old Testament. Here is our worship manual and hymnal, and it is as instructive as it is encouraging.

As God is worshiped as Creator in Revelation 4, so He is

worshiped as Redeemer in chapter 5. Our focus moves from the One upon the throne to the One who is hanging on the cross. The vision continues with John's gaze riveted on a scroll in God's right hand, "with writing on both sides and sealed with seven seals" (5:1). This "book of destiny" is in the firm grasp of the One upon the throne. The decrees of God are comprehensive and extensive, as the double-sided writing indicates. History is the unfolding of God's predetermined plan for all things. Chance and fate do not reign. God does!

John is further drawn into the drama of this worship as he sees and hears "a mighty angel [perhaps Gabriel] proclaiming in a loud voice, 'Who is worthy to break the seals and open the scroll?'" (5:2). That is, who could possibly be qualified "to perform the supreme service of bringing history to its foreordained consummation?"[2] But none could be found worthy of such a task from among the angels, or even the redeemed of the Lord. John weeps tears of pain as he confronts the whole people of God's unworthiness to even look inside the scroll, much less to open it.

An elder, representing redeemed mankind, responds, "Do not weep! See, the Lion of the tribe of Judah, the Root of David, has triumphed. He is able to open the scroll and its seven seals" (5:5). As the Lion, Jesus is the true King who is paramount over all. His human lineage is traced through Judah (Heb. 7:14; 2 Sam. 7:13, 16; Isa. 9:6 ff; Luke 1:32 ff; Gen. 49:9).

But He who came after King David is also before him (Isa. 11:1, 10; John 8:57 ff; Mic. 5:2; Rev. 22:16). In the birth of Jesus, the "Shoot of Jesse" is also revealed as the "Root of Jesse." He *alone* is worthy to open the scroll and its seven seals! As John Stott says, "Apart from the redeeming work of Jesus Christ, history is an enigma."[3]

John looks for a Lion and, instead, sees a Lamb. What a

glorious paradox! This Lamb—"looking as if it had been slain, standing in the center of the throne" (5:6)—becomes the central figure. Even in heaven we will be eternally reminded of the fact that it is only by virtue of Jesus' substitutionary atonement that we are there. He is the Messianic King because He has been faithful to His calling as the Lamb of God.

This is no ordinary lamb, but one with "seven horns" and "seven eyes." The "seven horns" do not need to be painted onto the image of a lamb. Instead, they are intended to make us think of the fullness of Jesus' power, as "horns" are a symbol of strength in the Scriptures (Deut. 33:17; Ps. 18:2; 1 Kings 22:11). This Lamb is the omnipotent Son of God! His "seven eyes" symbolize both His omniscience and the pervasiveness of His Spirit's work throughout creation. The Holy Spirit is the Spirit of Jesus (Rev. 1:4; Acts 16:7; Rom. 8:9).

In one of the most dramatic and glorious events in all of history, Jesus, as the Lamb, comes and takes the scroll from the Father's right hand. Immediately worship breaks out as the four living creatures and the twenty-four elders fall down before the Lamb (5:8). Each elder has a harp and holds golden bowls full of incense, "which are the prayers of the saints" (5:8). This tender picture reminds us that our supplications and our praises actually matter to God. The worship and prayers of the "church militant" connect us with the "church triumphant" like nothing else (Ex. 30:1–8; Deut. 33:10; Ps. 141:2; Luke 1:10).

Try to imagine experiencing what John was next privileged to witness. As the Lamb takes the scroll from our Father's hand the elders begin singing a "new song." This song of redemption is "new" in the sense that it is fresh and special. It is "a song that will never grow old because the wonder and joy of this salvation will never pall."[4] The

threefold worth of the Lamb to open the scroll is proclaimed
as He is praised.

- "You were slain" (5:9). Jesus' sacrificial death is the
zenith and purest expression of His costly and unconditional love for sinners.
- "You purchased men for God from every tribe and language and people and nation" (5:9). Jesus did not
merely make redemption possible. He has actually
secured the salvation of many from every people group.
- "You have made them to be a kingdom and priests to
serve our God, and they will reign on the earth" (5:10).
Through Jesus our lives have meaning, not just in eternity, but also in Tennessee, Asia Minor, throughout the
world, and throughout history.

What is the only appropriate response to such a glorious vision? John "looked and heard the voice of many
angels, numbering thousands upon thousands, and ten
thousand times ten thousand. They encircled the throne and
the living creatures and the elders. In a loud voice they sang:
'Worthy is the Lamb, who was slain, / to receive power and
wealth and wisdom and strength / and honor and glory and
praise!'" (5:11–12). What a dynamic and dramatic scene!
When is the last time you participated in a worship service
that approached this kind of inviting reality?

But this celebration of God's mercy and might grows even
grander. "Then I heard every creature in heaven and on earth
and under the earth and on the sea, and all that is in them,
singing: 'To him who sits on the throne and to the Lamb / be
praise and honor and glory and power, / for ever and ever!'
The four living creatures said, 'Amen,' and the elders fell
down and worshiped" (5:13–14). Everyone and everything

gives God and the Lamb their worthy due. Has a more awesome worship gathering ever been described?

What effect do you think this vision would have had on the seven churches in Asia Minor? The persecuted are deeply encouraged to endure all things on behalf of Him who bore all things for their redemption. The coldhearted are invited to be renewed in their affections for Him whose love is their own rebuke. Jewish Christians are secured in this new covenant faith as they are reassured that Jesus is, indeed, God's Messiah, the Lion of the tribe of Judah. The fearful are given strength, confidence, and hope as they see who really controls history and their destiny. The outnumbered Christians in the Roman world are made aware that they are far from being a minority, or they are a part of an uncountable community. Those deceived by false teaching are confronted with worship that is "in truth" and, therefore, pure. The small house churches in Asia Minor realize that when they gather to worship God they are a part of something far more majestic and immense than they could ever dream or imagine. The whole Church is called to affirm afresh, with confidence, passion, and joy, that Jesus, not Domitian, is *dominus et deus*, Lord and God.

What about us? How are we to be affected by the vision of heavenly worship given in Revelation? For those who claim great interest, passionate concern, and/or personal responsibility for the worship of God in our day, this portion of Scripture is critical and compelling. Doesn't it stand to reason that the perfected worship of heaven should be the paradigm from which we work as we seek to faithfully adore, praise, and honor the One who alone is worthy of everything that we have and are? How should our understanding and experience of worship in our church families be shaped by what we see of God's worship in eternity?

These are questions that I started asking the core group of our young church even before we assembled for our first worship service in Christ Community. When we planted our church, we stated unequivocally that the worship of the Triune God is to be our highest priority and our greatest joy. We also made an appeal for everyone called to be a part of our church family to surrender his worship agenda for God's. "Let's purpose to cultivate a worshiping community whose single reason for being is to bring glory to God through God-centered worship and living." This remains our passion to this day.

In our first year, I preached and taught on the topic of worship more than any other. As we give careful attention to the details of John's description in Revelation 4 and 5, certain "continuums of worship," which are instructive and helpful, emerged. These are the truths that guide us as we continue to seek to mature a generation as a community of God's people who accept the worship of God as our most glorious, important, and eternal of all callings. As Christians we are to accept what the Reformers called the "regulative principle," the belief that the Bible alone has the authority to regulate all things for the people of God, including what we do in worship. Perhaps in recent years we have unwittingly done a better job of worshiping worship than worshiping God. For as long as the discussion about worship centers on what we "like" or "dislike," we have missed the heart of worship. The questions we should be faithfully wrestling with are:

- "What does God desire in His worship?"
- "What is acceptable worship, according to the instruction we find in the Bible?"

- "How can we more faithfully represent, honor, and serve God in His worship?"

That we enjoy worshiping our Triune Lord is great, appropriate, and awesome! We should. But that is neither the point nor the goal of true worship. All that should ultimately matter to us is His glory and honor.

What follows in this chapter is a brief stating of some of the worship principles that we in Christ Community have learned from the book of Revelation and, indeed, from the whole Bible. These are the things that we constantly refer to in our church family as we seek to surrender our preferences to His purposes. Please be encouraged to seriously consider where you and your church family are with respect to worship as it is celebrated in heaven.

Continuums of Worship in Revelation

Spirit	Truth
(Holy Spirit) •————————————•	(Doctrine)

Many Christians tend to set up an unbiblical dichotomy based on the difference between what they call "dead worship" and "alive worship." "Dead worship" is usually stereotyped as being too cerebral, "liturgical," theological, weighty, musically "out of touch," and boring. "Alive worship" is described in terms of being "Spirit-led," emotionally real and affective, musically relevant, and "powerful." It is assumed, by many, that theology and passion are mutually exclusive in worship. But in the visions of worship given in Revelation, we find rich theology leading to impassioned doxology; sound doctrine effecting spiritual delight; a clearer vision of God segueing into a deeper experience of His glory and grace.

This same John who recorded Jesus' revelation of heavenly worship also recorded some of the most important teaching our Lord gave on the topic of worship. In chapter 4 of John's gospel Jesus had an amazing encounter with a Samaritan woman in which He made known to her ". . . a time is coming and has now come when the true worshipers will worship the Father in spirit and truth, for they are the kind of worshipers the Father seeks" (John 4:23). It is important for us to hear in Jesus' words that, first of all, our Father is seeking worshipers. It should humble us to realize that our God actually longs for and delights in the worship of His people.

Second, however, notice that not just any kind of worship will do. True worship (as opposed to unacceptable worship) must be "in spirit *and* in truth." Neither "dead orthodoxy" (truth without Spirit) nor "live heterodoxy" (Spirit without truth) is acceptable to God. God's worship must be grounded in His truth and enlivened by His Spirit. This balanced continuum must be celebrated in every liturgical setting in the Christian church, no matter if our ecclesiastical heritage is Episcopal, Charismatic, Baptist, nondenominational, Presbyterian, Vineyard, House Church, or whatever. As I was once instructed, "All truth and no Spirit, we dry up. All Spirit and no truth, we blow up. Spirit and truth, we grow up."

Our church family is comprised of believers from many different theological backgrounds. It has been very encouraging to watch those who come from a largely experience-based view of the Christian life develop a love for the truth of the Scriptures as the foundation for all spiritual experience. And it has been equally heartening to watch those who come from a more didactic and dogmatic background begin to "thaw out" and experience the implications of the great truths they have been so disciplined to learn and protect.

Transcendence   •————————•   **Immanence**
(God's Holiness)   **(God's Nearness)**

God's "holy otherness" is celebrated in John's visions just as His "Abba," Father's, heart is fully enjoyed. We hear the same "Holy, holy, holy" ringing out in the worship of heaven as Isaiah experienced his magnificent vision (Isaiah 6). God is "high and lifted up." His glory still fills the temple. John also describes God coming off His exalted throne and wiping every tear out of the eyes of the people of God! What a glorious mixture of images! What a juxtaposition of reverence and intimacy. Every generation of Christians, however, tends to negate one of these aspects of God's Being in preference for the other, but we are not to treat the attributes of God like ice cream from which we pick our "flavor of choice."

Such an attitude is what the Bible calls idolatry, the remaking of God after our own image or liking. However, we dare not trivialize the worship of God by reducing it to some kind of a syrupy sentimental familiarity. And neither are we worshiping faithfully, and in keeping with His own self-revelation, when we keep God in the rafters of the cathedral under the pretense of "mystery" and respect. In heaven, we will fully and eternally enjoy an affectionate reverence for God. May the same become increasingly manifest in the way we worship Him today.

As I write this book, I am reflecting on where our church family is in this very important continuum. For our first ten years, as a community of recovering legalists and Pharisees, we have learned so much about the mercy, grace, and love of God. We richly enjoy God's nearness in the gospel. May that never change! I sense, however, that our Father has much more to teach us about His holiness and glory. I am looking forward to our entering into a new season of rediscovering what it means to be in awe of God's majesty and eternal perfections. Without such a vision, God's people have tended to trivialize the gospel of God's grace. May that never happen to us.

Mind (Noetic) •————————• **Body (Somatic)**

"Whole person" worship is very obvious in heaven. Those who ponder the richness of theology with their eyes, ears, and minds are falling off their thrones in bodily response. They stand, wave palm branches, and sing loudly of God's glory and grace. In the late sixties and early seventies I was right in the middle of many of the "worship wars" that ensued as the Jesus Movement began to impact mainline evangelical churches. I look back now with some embarrassment at how petty and immature many of us were as we debated such "weighty" issues as whether pipe organs or guitars were more pleasing to God in corporate worship.

Another topic of great interest, which generated considerable concern, was whether or not it was appropriate to "lift hands" in public worship. Whole churches were divided over this issue! How sad. I remember a question-and-answer session I attended in seminary, in which Dr. J. I. Packer was asked, "Dr. Packer, what do you think about all of these emotional people coming into our churches and lifting their hands, falling to their knees, and drawing attention to themselves?"

I will never forget his response. "My dear brother," he said with pastoral sensitivity and yet fatherly authority, "the question is not whether we should kneel in our worship services today. The question is, shall we who will kneel one day kneel now as well?" Bingo! That settled the issue for me. Though not mandated, it is quite appropriate for us to lift our hands, to kneel, to prostrate ourselves, to respond with our whole person to the whole gospel. Because we have dealt with this issue from the Scriptures in a very up-front way, we enjoy great freedom and we show loving respect for one another in our church family.

Let us use our minds to the glory of God *and* let us present our bodies as living sacrifices. May raised hands in worship be a sign of raised theological understanding. The two complement one another.

Vertical •————————• Horizontal

In the visions of heaven in Revelation we also find the perfect balance between the vertical God-centeredness of worship and the horizontal celebration by the great sea of redeemed humanity. God is in the center of all things. He is the focus. His is the glory. Worship is perfectly in the round. But the emanating concentric circles are meant to remind us that worship is not about *you* and it's not about *me*. It's about *us*, the twice-reconciled people of God. Our Father has reconciled us to Himself and to each other. Both of these relationships are to be demonstrated and celebrated as we worship.

We dare not privatize or provincialize that which is meant to free us from all forms of self-preoccupation and self-interest. Indeed, there is nothing more personal and intimate than worship, but the worship of heaven reminds us that we are a part of the growing orchestra of praise that God is building from every race, tribe, tongue, and nation.

In each of our worship celebrations at Christ Community,

I encourage our church family primarily to "look up." Our focus is on our Triune God. But we also "look around." We greet each other not just to be sociable or Southern, but to be biblical. Ninety-nine percent of the imperatives in the Bible are plural. The worship of God is wondrously personal but it is not to be viewed as a private event. We are "living stones" that are being joined with others to become a "spiritual house" for the purpose of offering "spiritual sacrifices acceptable to God through Jesus Christ" (1 Peter 2:5). Our generation of Christians needs *desperately* to rediscover the implications of our calling to corporate worship.

Diversity ●————● Unity

That this great community of the redeemed maintains their "every people" identity in heaven is instructive as we ponder the importance of both diversity and unity. It is tragic, indeed, for us to seek to be overly homogeneous in our worship experience. Diversity should be intentional, not accidental. Unity must not be confused with uniformity. Nothing has had a more positive effect on the maturing of the worship in Christ Community than our being willing to "risk rather than rust" in terms of deploying the diversity of gifts that God has deposited among us. Every one of us has been stretched!

The Scriptures do not mandate every local expression of the body of Christ to look just alike, for we need a diversity of churches in any given community for the purpose of outreach into all cultural contexts. However, the gospel mandates that every church be very careful to draw a liturgical circle big enough to celebrate all the distinctive elements within that particular community of the redeemed: young and old, male and female, rich and poor, the washed and the unwashed, "old guard" and new transplants, the traditional and the contemporary. The gospel is God's gracious work of reconciliation, and His worship is to reflect how this reconciliation is celebrated in every relational context of life. Let us learn to respect and celebrate one another's gifts now as a foretaste of how we will richly enjoy one another in the worship of heaven.

Heart (Inner Expression) ←———————→ Art (Outward Expression)

As you look very carefully at the worship of heaven you will realize that it includes many elements that are spatial, visual, auditory, musical, participatory, dialogical, just to name a few. These represent the *art* of heavenly worship and should be seen as the creative expression of the *heart* of worship.

God bids us surrender our creative energies, gifts, and artistic sensibilities to the most noble and grand of all events and realities, the worship of God. No, we are not called to worship art nor artists, for this is nothing more than idolatry. (Tragically, the church has proven itself quite capable of this and many other idolatries in our worship services.) But neither are we to congratulate ourselves for giving artless expression to the riches of our theology and experience of the living God. Too often we settle for a "hymn sandwich" in our worship services: a big, fat slice of meaty sermon between an opening and closing hymn. Surely God's worship is to be more creative and participatory than this! As a pastor who loves to teach, I have had to repent of an unbalanced view of how much time I demand for my "preachment" in the worship service. The ministry of the Word is still prominent, but it is not exclusive to the other vital elements of biblical worship.

There is more of a defense for "artless" worship than there is for "heartless" worship. Shall we offer to the Lord that which costs us nothing? A commitment to the art of worship led our elders to create a position called director of worship ministries. There is no staff position in our church that is more important. This individual is called to work, pray, study, and plan with me concerning the cultivation of God's worship in our fellowship. We are enjoying watching God lead us from lightweight worship into that which is at least a shadow of what awaits us in heaven. How weighty, how creative, how glorious!

Liturgy •————————• Life

Lastly, we should be profoundly stirred by the implications of God being worshiped in Revelation 4 as Creator before He is worshiped in chapter 5 as Redeemer. The whole of life is to be seen as the "worship center" for the people of God. His praise is to be demonstrated and celebrated in all of life, in all of His world, in every sphere of His creation. Indeed, we are to plan, pray, and work hard at cultivating faithful worship in our weekly celebrations in terms of the liturgy, the Word, prayers, sacraments, and music. But we must not reduce worship to mean only that which occurs in the sanctuary one hour a week.

Such reductionism has been destructive to the way God's people tend to think of the nature of worship. *All* of life, for Christians, is to be lived as an act of worship. The chief end of man is "to glorify God and to enjoy Him forever." We do this best when we seek to worship Him in every sphere of life: work, play, family, friendship. Everywhere, all the time.

William Temple, the founder and president of Temple University, offered a very helpful definition of worship that captures this comprehensive and consuming understanding of worship:

> Worship is the submission of all our nature to God. It is the quickening of conscience by His holiness; the nourishment of mind with His truth; the purifying of imagination by His beauty; the opening of the heart to His love; the surrender of will to His purpose—and all this gathered up in adoration, the most selfless emotion of which our nature is capable and therefore the chief remedy for that self-centeredness which is our original sin and the source of all actual sin.[5]

As it is in heaven, may it be incrementally and demonstrably so here!

THE SONG OF THE LAMB

Revelation 5: 9–10

FROM THE SONG

In the course of writing the series of songs contained in this book, I made a surprising discovery. I had set out to analyze what I always thought of as the "hymn fragments" contained in the Revelation. I outlined their positions in the text as well as their various themes. Long after I had thought my analysis was complete, it occurred to me to look at the statements that prefaced the "hymns" so I could determine what kind of treatment they would receive musically (choral, solo). To my surprise, most of the fragments were not prefaced by "and they *sang*" but by "they shouted in a loud voice," or simply, "said."

Out of the approximately thirteen "hymns" (depending on how you count them) only two are said to have been sung, one by the elders in chapter 5, the other by those who are described as "victorious" in chapter 15. (There is another scene in chapter 14 in which the 144,000 sing a song, known only to them, but John does not record these words for us.)

If we were to adopt the worship pattern from Revelation, only one in six songs would be sung in our congregations. The others would be "acclamations." They would be said in unison or very likely "shouted" together. We don't shout at God enough!

Peterson, in his wonderful book *Reversed Thunder*[6] describes Revelation as a book of worship. If he is right, then once again the Bible has stretched our narrow definition. All too often we settle for songs when the Word would have us sing, say, even shout to God, all in the process of offering ourselves to Him as living sacrifices (Rom. 12:1).

This is the single song in Revelation (for which the words are recorded) which also speaks of harps, and one of only two designated as having been "sung." (It is from this single verse that the tired image of sitting on a cloud in heaven, strumming your harp is derived.) If by nothing but the title alone, we should regard this as the most important "song" in the book; the "Song of the Lamb."

At first I sought a classical, "Handelesque" approach: large symphony and choir giving it all they had. But the more I actually listened to the text, the more a poignancy about the words, which didn't seem to fit the treatment I had in mind, surfaced. Even amidst the joy, there is a brokenheartedness, for there are yet the seven terrible bowls of God's wrath to come.

And so I sat down at my own harp and began to strum through a few chords. To my surprise, the verses, which describe the scene, seemed to be best set in a minor key with the chorus resolving to the major—though still a somewhat sad major.

Doesn't all real joy, even the joy of heaven—perhaps especially the joy of heaven—contain at its heart a twinge, a bit of black satin cloth against which the diamond of joy seems especially beautiful? When we stand at last before the Lamb, still bearing His healing wounds, will we not—amidst the inexpressible joy—think back to His suffering, to the suffering of our tired old world, or even to our own suffering?

"You are the Lamb that was slain!" will be our shout—our word of praise. You, our blessed, meek, glorious Servant, suffered for this moment! And so we will surely glory over His woundedness—and perhaps weep because of it. But compared to the joy, the tears will seem as a drop in the great blue ocean of God's eternal joy; and those tears (if indeed there be tears) will be gently wiped away. It's a promise.

The Song of the Lamb

Victorious army
With God-given harps in their hands
By a sea set on fire
They all sing the Song of the Lamb.

Just and true are your ways,
King of Ages,
Great and marvelous are all your deeds,
Oh, Lord God Almighty.
Who will not fear You?
And bring glory to Your Name?

A temple in heaven
And angels with bowls in their hands
Smoke and glory
And the power of God to command.

Just and true are your ways,
King of Ages;
Great and marvelous are all your deeds,
Oh, Lord God Almighty.
Who will not fear You
And bring glory to Your Name?

Yes, Lord God Almighty,
Your judgments are true.
They've slain saints and prophets,
Now give them their due.

CHAPTER FIVE

REVELATION 5:9–10
THE HOPE OF A
COMPLETED "GREAT COMMISSION"

FROM THE WORD

Call me strange, weird, or worse, but ever since I became a Christian I have had little if any zeal for taking a trip to Israel. I have always preferred the idea of tracing the roots of the Reformation through Western Europe or even sailing among the Greek Isles to relive the missionary journeys of the apostle Paul. I guess that which has fueled my "holy land aversion" more than anything else is my fear of commercialization. The thought of having someone offering to sell me a splinter of the "original" Noah's ark or one of the pebbles David may have used to kill Goliath or a little piece of the large stone which sealed Jesus' tomb . . . I think you get the picture.

Another reason I have been slow to respond to the many opportunities afforded me to tour the "land of Moses and Jesus" is because of a conviction that I developed in graduate school. I remember one of my professors of biblical theology asking the class why we evangelicals customarily refer to Israel as "the holy land." At first, I was somewhat taken aback by his query. I thought to myself, *Any dummy knows the answer to that question. It's the "holy land" because that's what God calls it in the Bible*. But then I had a hard time—no, an impossible time—finding a single chapter and verse in the Scriptures like that.

The point this outstanding teacher made changed my whole worldview. As Christians, we are to see the *entire* earth as the "holy land." Every square inch of terra firma, even the parts of creation that we cannot see, are made by and for Jesus. One day the knowledge of the glory of the Lord is going to fill the *whole* earth as the waters cover the sea! My vision had been way too small.

It is true that many of the great acts of God in the history of redemption have occurred in the land of Israel. And the Scriptures tell us that more mighty acts of God are to be revealed there. It most definitely is an important piece of real estate for anyone who takes the Bible seriously. But in the Scriptures, especially in the book of Revelation, the concept of "the land" gives way to the ultimate theme of "a new heavens and a new earth," the final reality that Jesus will usher in at His second coming. Until our Lord returns, however, we are to be excited about the expanding work of the Kingdom of God, which is being effected throughout the world, in *every* sphere of life, among all the nations of the world. "Of the increase of His government and peace there will be *no* end" (Isa. 9:7, emphasis mine).

Holy Land or Hollywood?

I finally made my first trip to Israel in the spring of 1995. And yes, some of my stereotypes were confirmed (including a chapel built over the rock which Jesus "obviously" used to step onto the back of the donkey which He rode into Jerusalem to make His triumphant entry!). All things considered, however, I am glad I went, and I will go again.

Among the many memories and images etched into my

heart from that first trip, none is more enduring than the visit our group took to the Garden Tomb at the Hill of the Skull. This is one of the two main locations that archaeologists believe to be the place where Jesus was crucified, buried, and raised from the dead. The tomb of Jesus is nestled in a beautifully manicured garden park, which is preserved as a ministry, directed and overseen by a group of very gracious Christians from Great Britain.

Even though we cannot know for sure (until heaven) which was the real site of the crucifixion, burial, and resurrection of Jesus, there is a strong possibility that this is the actual site. The main point, however, is that we realize that biblical faith is grounded in things that really occurred in "time and in space," as Francis Schaeffer used to emphasize over and over. To visit Israel is to get the sense of that history. As Christians, we are not just another group of mystics who invented "religious myths" to serve the purposes of our esoteric spirituality.

In one of his earlier works the apostle John wrote, "That which was from the beginning, which we have heard, which we have seen with our eyes, which we have looked at and our hands have touched—this we proclaim concerning the Word of life" (1 John 1:1). John stressed the physical reality of the incarnation of Jesus. Likewise, the apostle Paul said, "If Christ has not been raised, our preaching is useless and so is your faith . . . And if Christ has not been raised, your faith is futile; you are still in your sins. Then those also who have fallen asleep in Christ are lost. If only for this life we have hope in Christ, we are to be pitied more than all men. But Christ has indeed been raised from the dead, the firstfruits of those who have fallen asleep" (1 Cor. 15:14, 17–20). To go to Israel is to gain a profound sense that the stories of the Bible are not just theological "Aesop's Fables."

The Garden of Grace

As we walked through the beautifully cultivated and cared for garden my heart began to rejoice. Perhaps with the doubting heart of Thomas I found myself saying with greater conviction, "It's true, it's really true. I can see it. I can touch it. Jesus did die on the cross for *my* sins. He was buried and raised from the dead, for *me!* This may very well be the place where it all happened."

Our informed and gracious guide, a retiree from London, led us to the location where our Nashville family was to celebrate the Lord's Supper. Every Christian group is given the privilege of having a worship service and communion before leaving these much beloved grounds. There is *nothing* that had a greater impact on me during our entire travels throughout the land of Israel.

As we gathered in a little open-air chapel area and sang hymns of praise and several Scripture choruses, many of which came to us from the text of Revelation, we realized that we were far from alone. All around us were groups, perhaps ten or more, who were doing exactly the same thing, glorying in the love and grace of the One who gave Himself for the forgiveness of all of our sins. No two groups were from the same nation! There were Filipinos, Australians, Koreans, Germans, Dutch, and Irish just to name a few. Everyone was worshiping Jesus in his own language, with hands and hearts raised in glad adoration of our One Savior. This became a foretaste, better still, the firstfruits of heaven to my soul.

A Full and Multinational Heaven

Immediately I thought of John's vision of heaven and especially his recording of the "new song" that he heard filling up the sanctuary of eternity, "You are worthy to take the scroll / and to open its seals, / because you were slain, / and with your blood you purchased men for God / from every tribe and language and people and nation. / You have made them to be a kingdom and priests to serve our God, / and they will reign on the earth" (5:9–10).

As I heard the many tribes, languages, peoples, and nations in the Garden Tomb, I couldn't help but ponder what effect this vision would have had on the first-century church. We are alive after twenty centuries of the advance of the gospel throughout so much of the world and world history, but what about the persecuted church in Asia Minor? How would they have interpreted such a vision? *Has John lost his mind?* they might have thought. *Is he exercising apostolic hyperbole? Maybe he's just bringing a little encouragement before Rome wipes out Christians and the young church from the face of the earth.*

Nonsense! John's vision of heaven overflowing with men and women from every people group is to be understood in light of the covenant that God made with His servant Abram, recorded in the book of Genesis. "The LORD had said to Abram, 'Leave your country, your people and your father's household and go to the land I will show you. I will make you into a great nation / and I will bless you; / I will make your name great, / and you will be a blessing. / I will bless those who bless you, / and whoever curses you I will curse; / and *all peoples on earth* / will be blessed through you'" (Gen. 12:1–3, emphasis mine). God sovereignly took a pagan from Ur of the Chaldeans, reconciled him to Himself through an act of sheer grace, and then gave him exceeding great and glorious promises, which can only be fulfilled by God Himself!

A Meta-Vision

How fitting it is then for the Bible to end with a vision of the fulfillment of this awesome promise made to the one who would be renamed Abraham, "father of nations." The entire Bible, from Genesis through Revelation, is the unfolding and recording of the history of redemption, God's sovereign promise and plan to redeem for Himself a people from *every* people group from *every* period in the history of mankind. It has always been God's intent to use Israel as a means of accomplishing His larger saving purposes among *all* the nations of the world.

Persecuted Christians in Asia Minor must have been stunned and encouraged as they had this vision read to them for the first time. They were reminded that God has not forgotten His covenant. He will not forsake His people. The church is not going to die a quick death with a meager membership of converted Jews and a small smattering of Gentiles. Rome and all of the hoards of evil will not prevail.

Not only will the church survive the first-century persecutions, she will thrive until the very day when Jesus comes back to receive His completed bride unto Himself. We cannot emphasize this encouraging promise too much: Heaven *will be* full of men and women from *every* tribe, language, people, and nation. Such an image caused "ten thousand times ten thousand" angels to join the living creatures and the elders in singing in a loud voice, "Worthy is the Lamb, who was slain, / to receive power and wealth and wisdom and strength / and honor and glory and praise!" (5:12).

This magnificent end of history is no mere possibility or probability. It will be an actuality, for Jesus, as the sacrificial Lamb of God, has already "purchased men for God" by the atonement He accomplished through His death on the cross. A legal transaction has been effected between Jesus and God the Father. Redemption has been accomplished and now it is being sovereignly applied to the nations of the world!

The death of Jesus Christ upon the cross did not merely make salvation *possible* for any who would receive it. Rather, it is the *guarantee* of salvation to "the many" for whom He gave His life. The book of Revelation is not a book of mere possibilities. It is the triumphant shout, the glad declaration that the Lamb has triumphed over sin and death! He will not be denied. Jesus has come not just to offer salvation to the interested but "to seek and to save the lost."

The "Great Commission": Job or Joy?

How our generation of Christians needs to have a renewed vision and confidence in the cross of Jesus and what He accomplished there. The Great Commission is a restating of God's promise to Abraham, and it is our privilege, as the church, to enter in to the prepared harvest.

Jesus has been given all authority "in heaven and on earth." He is with us till the end of the age and He is going to have disciples from among "all nations." We see this great expectation celebrated as we read through the book of Acts. The gospel spreads from Jerusalem, through Judea, to Samaria, and to the uttermost parts of the earth.

The implications of this hope should be obvious for the Church of Jesus Christ. Evangelism and missions should be central and not tangential to everything that we do. We are not just to have a missions program. We are to see ourselves, the whole church, as part of a missionary movement! As Rhienhold Neibhur said, "As fire exists by burning so the Church exists by missions." The main reason that our Lord Jesus has yet to return to this world is because God's work of redeeming His people from among the nations is not finished.

Until the return of Jesus we are to exist as a missionary people; for, as the apostle Peter refers to the Church, "You are a chosen people, a royal priesthood, a holy nation, a people belonging to God, that you may declare the praises of him who called you out of darkness into his wonderful light. Once you were not a people, but now you are the people of God; once you had not received mercy, but now you have received mercy" (1 Pet. 2:9–10). As we declare the praises of God among the nations of the world, He effectually calls His people to life in Christ.

The more I meditate upon the missionary promises found throughout the Bible, the more I see the relationship between worship and missions. As we lift up the name of Jesus, our Father draws those who are being saved unto Himself.

We are like Gideon's army going against the Midianites, David against Goliath, or Elijah against the four hundred prophets of Baal. The odds seem overwhelming, the challenge enormous. We dare not go forth into world evangelism in our own strength. Rather, we are those who, like the apostle Paul, acknowledge that "we have this treasure in jars of clay to show that this all-surpassing power is from God and not from us" (2 Cor. 4:7). "For we are to God the aroma of Christ among those who are being saved and those who are perishing. To the one we are the smell of death; to the other, the fragrance of life. And who is equal to such a task? . . . our competence comes from God" (2 Cor. 2:15–16; 3:5).

Spanish Gypsies

My mentor, Jack Miller, taught me much about the power of weakness and the joy of entering into the secured harvest. Because of this vision of a full and multinational heaven, Jack was a dangerous man! I will never forget one phone call he made to me several years ago. "Scotty, this is Jack. What are you and Darlene doing this September? I have a little trip in mind for us."

Oh, no, I thought to myself, *Jack's up to it again.*

He continued, "I would love for you and your sweet wife to come with Rose Marie and a few of us to Spain."

Remembering that Spain was the country where Jack loved to go for rest and relaxation, I breathed easier. I envisioned a retreat to the hills of southern Spain for a small group of Jack and Rose Marie's children in the faith where we'd spend our time reading, praying, enjoying the grandeur of the Mediterranean, the aged vintage of the vineyards, and the sweet fellowship of a few other Christians. It sounded great! I felt "chosen" and special! But then Jack continued.

"Yes, Scotty, I've been praying and the Lord has put on my heart the gypsies of southern Spain. I think we should go into the gypsy camps and tell them about the love and grace of Jesus. We would love for the two of you to come and join us. What do you think?"

"Sounds, er, uh, great, Jack," I shot back with all the enthusiasm of someone "looking forward" to having their wisdom teeth cut out with a dull butter knife. For some reason the combination of "gypsies" and "grace" seemed like an oxymoron.

As you can imagine, we went to Spain, and a life-impacting experience it was. Our little community of grace made its way, with much weakness and fear, into a couple of gypsy camps to sing God's praises; to share the gospel in our very broken Spanish; and to rely on the love that God has for us.

One evening while we were in Malaga, a very humble Venezuelan pastor took us to a church made up of converted gypsies. I have never seen a greater example of the power of the gospel to change anyone, anywhere. Oh, the joy, the glow, the reality, the praises to God that were offered by a culturally despised people whose very name is slang for "deceitful and wicked!" What we witnessed was John's vision of the fulfilled Great Commission, God's covenant of redemption in real life. *Every* people group will be represented in heaven, even Spanish gypsies! This is true not because we are going to "get the job done," but because the Lamb has purchased men for God! All praise be to our God of all grace!

John's Joy and Ours

This vision of a full heaven has proven to be the driving force and power behind the history of the contemporary missions movement. May our own hearts be deeply encouraged to enter into the prepared harvest as we anticipate the day when we will gather around the throne of grace with our brothers and sisters from every tribe, language, people, and nation to worship Him who paid the full price for our salvation, Jesus, the Lamb of God.

This harvest is all around us: in the gypsy camps of Spain, in our own homes, neighborhoods, offices, among Roman centurions, "skinheads," liberal Democrats and right-wing Republicans, in Iraq, and in the Bible Belt. There is *no* place where people are outside of the saving purposes of our God—except hell itself.

CHAPTER SIX

REVELATION 6:1–8:1
THE HOPE OF
PURPOSEFUL SUFFERING

FROM THE WORD

kay, let's pretend you are reading the book of Revelation for the very first time. You have read through the first three chapters and say to yourself, *So far, so good. What's the big fuss? This isn't so confusing. It's about Jesus and His loving concern for His bride, the church.* Then you read chapters 4 and 5, and even though much of the imagery seems rather strange, there is still a sense that Revelation is not such a formidable and unfriendly part of the Bible. In fact, your heart is actually encouraged and stirred as you ponder the inviting sights and sounds of the throne room vision. *Maybe it doesn't take a seminary education to "crack the code" to the Apocalypse, after all,* you conclude with much relish and relief.

But then you resume your reading at chapter 6 and before long, you hit the "Revelation wall." Lost in the mire of "seals," "trumpets," and "woes," you are tempted to run back to the safe and predictable harbors of the Gospel of John or the book of Psalms. A retreat into the more familiar parts of the Bible is all the more inviting because a myriad of experts seem to speak with such confidence and authority concerning the "obvious" meaning of each number, image, sound, animal, and weather change—from chapter 6 all the way through chapter 22. Yet, there is so little consensus among the interpreters about what each detail actually means. That is why so many Christians just give up trying to understand this most encouraging book.

Assumptions or Presumptions?

What you just read is my own story. For the first ten years of my walk with the Lord, I could never move comfortably beyond chapter 5 of Revelation. I had the hardest time trying to make everything fit sequentially into an understandable time line. And most of the charts, books, and tapes I was exposed to seemed to be rather contrived and sensational. To make matters worse, the first whole Bible I owned came replete with a system of interpretation printed at the bottom of each page, which was harder to make sense of than the Scriptures themselves! But to a young believer, if it's in the Bible, it must be true, and that includes the notes! How did I know that these weren't the apostle John's own Bible study notations?

It's amazing what you learn when you are preparing to teach through a whole book of the Bible for the very first time! How I thank God for the faithful and inquisitive men and women of Christ Community Church who forced me to look a lot deeper into the structure of Revelation as we set our hearts to understand this book of hope together.

Before giving serious critical attention to the Apocalypse, I just assumed that it followed a simple chronological order. That is, I figured Revelation was written along a historical time line from chapter to chapter. This was, I thought, especially the case when we come to chapters 6 through 22. For example: the breaking of the seven seals would precede the blowing of the seven trumpets, which would precede the pouring forth of the seven bowls of God's wrath. At the end of these three chronological cycles of seven, Jesus would then return and the world, as we know it, would come to an end. This seemed so logical, so reasonable.

The problem came, however, when I began to notice that the second coming of Jesus, and events relegated in the Scriptures to the end of all things, occurred in all three of these cycles! In fact, the second coming seems to occur six or seven times after the breaking of the first seal!

Perhaps what we have here is similar to what we see in the four gospels. As we read Matthew, Mark, Luke, and John it becomes obvious that the life, ministry, and work of our Lord Jesus are told from four different perspectives. There are no contradictions among the four, just different emphases, given the personality and calling of each author. When we study all four of the gospel writers, we get a much fuller understanding of the one true Gospel. Could it be that this is the way God has written the last book of the Bible? I am now convinced that the structure of Revelation is similar to that of a great wallpaper, as one author put it, with a distinctive-and-repetitive pattern. Or better yet, a great drama told in several vignettes, each telling the same story with a specific emphasis: the story of the "last days."

A "Last Days" Thriving Manual

But that leads us to another very important question that has implications for how we understand John's writing style: When are the "last days"? When I became a Christian in 1968, this question was front and center. In fact, it was actually a rhetorical question. It was assumed that we were living in the "last days." But it was also assumed that the "last days" only began rather recently, as in the beginning of the '60s.

According to the Scriptures, however, the "last days" have been going on for quite a while. The apostle Peter stood up on the Day of Pentecost and announced in one of the most important sermons ever preached, "These men are not drunk, as you suppose. It's only nine in the morning! No, this is what was spoken by the prophet Joel: 'In the last days, God says, / I will pour out my Spirit on all people'" (Acts 2:15–17). Peter, under the direction of the Holy Spirit, interpreted the events of the day as indicative of that period which the Old Testament prophets referred to as the "last days."

Likewise, the writer of the book of Hebrews gives us important insight into this final period in the history of redemption. "In the past God spoke to our forefathers through the prophets at many times and in various ways, but in these last days he has spoken to us by his Son, whom he appointed heir of all things, and through whom he made the universe" (Heb. 1:1–2). According to these two inspired authors of Scripture the "last days" actually began with the first coming of Jesus Christ and the outpouring of the Holy Spirit on the Day of Pentecost. The entire period between the first and second coming of Jesus should be viewed as the "last days."

Before writing Revelation the apostle John had already affirmed his belief that the first-century church was living in the "last days" when he wrote, "Dear children, this is the last hour; and as you have heard that the antichrist is coming, even now many antichrists have come. This is how we know it is the last hour" (1 John 2:18). So are we living in the "last days"? Absolutely! Are we living in the last of the "last days"? Let no man presume to know!

This leads me to assert that Revelation is a "last days"

thriving (not just surviving!) manual for the whole people of God. Each of the several scenes that are presented in Revelation 6–22 are "recapitulative vignettes," gracious gifts of God to His people; informing, warning, and encouraging us about things that have been, things that are, and things that are to come. The same events and time line are viewed from different perspectives with different emphases. In "computer speak," it is similar to clicking on to a particular icon for the sake of highlighting an important aspect of the whole. As we study each of these scenes in the drama of redemption, a more comprehensive picture of the Christian life emerges. Life between the comings of Christ is presented as being full of "rapture and rupture," and Jesus is thoroughly in control of all things, including the suffering of His people.

To help the men and women in our church family begin to see this repetitive pattern and structure in John's writing, I encouraged them to read Revelation 6:1–11:19 in one sitting. It was fun to watch the shackles of "Revelation confusion" begin to fall off! "Why haven't I ever seen this before?" "This makes a lot of sense, but are you sure, Scotty?" "My grandmother is going to get me for believing like this." "What am I going to do with my old reference Bible?"

The verses I had them read covers the breaking of the "seven seals" and the blowing of the "seven trumpets." The similarities between these two groups of seven are telling. The first four seals are opened at once; likewise, the first four trumpets are sounded together. Then the fifth and sixth seals are opened as a unit, just as the fifth and six trumpets are heralded as a unit. In similar fashion, before the breaking of the seventh seal and the blowing of the seventh trumpet, there is intermediate material and a vision that preserves the unity in the structure of John's writing.

New Testament scholar Bruce Metzger concludes from observing this pattern, "Thus, the seven seals and the seven trumpets essentially tell the same thing, each time emphasizing one or another aspect of the whole."[1] In light of this, I encouraged those who were studying with me to try reading Revelation 6–22 and Bunyan's spiritual classic, *Pilgrim's Progress*, at the same time. There are some striking similarities between the two. Both are, essentially, descriptions of the different dimensions of life for the people of God as we make our way to the "Celestial City." Both should be read not for the purpose of looking for signs and setting dates, but for the purpose of "growing in the grace and knowledge of our Lord and Savior, Jesus Christ."

Jesus Is the Lord of History

As we turn our attention to the first of these repetitive patterns, "the breaking of the seven seals," what does this vignette tell us about life between the first and second comings of Christ? (What "icon" is being clicked onto?)

I will never forget the evening I started teaching through this section of the Apocalypse. We reread chapter 5 as a prelude to our study of the "seven seals" in Revelation 6:1–8:1. Worship broke out as we rejoiced, once again, in the profoundly stirring vision of Jesus coming forward to open the book of destiny. The whole of history is under His dominion. History is, indeed, *His* story.

Life Is Hard But God Is Good

In Revelation 6:1–8 we have the breaking of the first four seals, each having a rider upon a different colored horse. As they come forth we see that each depicts catastrophic developments for the inhabitants of the earth under the sovereign hand of God. To be forewarned is to be forearmed. Our Father wants us to know that life on earth between the first and second comings of Christ is going to be very difficult at times. The "Four Horsemen of the Apocalypse" give us a vision of a world that is permeated by the effects of the Fall. These horsemen are riding forth today. John had already been given such a worldview as Jesus told the twelve disciples, "In this world you will have trouble. But take heart! I have overcome the world" (John 16:33).

If the persecuted Christians of the first-century church were at all perplexed or dismayed by what was going on all around them, these words would have come as a source of great comfort. God has not abandoned His people. Rome does not have the upper hand. Satan is not thwarting the eternal purposes of God. Here is an honest picture of what we can expect as we live the life of grace in a world in rebellion against God our Father.

My heart rejoiced as I began to see that the Bible is a lot more honest about life in the fallen world than I was led to believe.

For years I was exhorted to believe that if I had "enough faith," I could almost leap over tall buildings of adversity in a single bound; be faster than a speeding bullet through the difficulties of life; and be more powerful than a locomotive as I plowed through the negative into the positive dimensions of the "victorious Christian life." Call me "superman-Christian"! But call this "triumphalism," not, "the normal Christian life." Like most of us, I have a natural aversion to pain and suffering.

THE FIRST FOUR SEALS—LIFE IN A FALLEN WORLD

The First Seal—Rev. 6:1–2—Nations Warring Against Nations

Here we are given a picture of international warfare— nation against nation. As the white horse rides forth we see that tyranny, violence, and a lust for world dominion will characterize the whole period of life between the first and second comings of Christ. (Even a cursory reading of the history of mankind leads one to the same conclusion.) Christians will be caught in the cross fire and, in fact, will be in the middle of the battle, for we are God's army just as we are Christ's bride.

The Second Seal—Rev. 6:3–4—Brokenness in the Human Community

The tragedy of Cain and Abel will continue until Jesus returns, not just among nations but even in one's own household. Here is a picture of bloodshed among men, the tragic taking of one another's lives. Notice that this rider upon the red horse "was *given* power to take peace from the earth" (6:4, emphasis mine). God sets the parameters on the extent of the violence. Let not the first-century church, or the church of any century, despair. Our God reigns even over the manifestations of evil from the hearts of men.

The Third Seal—Rev. 6:5–6—Economic Chaos and Inequity

With the black horse come economic chaos and the uneven distribution of wealth and famine. "The rich will get richer and the poor will get poorer." Yet again, notice the limitations put on the gross injustice among mankind. "Do not damage the oil and the wine!" (6:6). These necessities of life, though affected by the greed of men, are protected by our God. Our Father will allow the evil devices of a world in rebellion against Him to go just so far. He, not they, is in ultimate control of all things, including the realm of food and money.

The Fourth Seal—Rev. 6:7–8—Death by Many Means

As the fourth seal is broken, a pale horse comes forth with an ominous rider, Death is his name, "and Hades was following close behind him." (6:8). Yet, as we have already seen, Jesus is the master over "death and Hades" (Rev. 1:18). Let us be warned, but let us not fear. This seal represents death by unexpected causes for "a fourth" of those upon the earth. There is nothing to indicate that this number is relegated to a period just before the return of Jesus. Rather, tragic death by all sorts of means will be experienced by a significant minority in the world until the "grave robber," Jesus, returns for His people.

THE FIFTH AND SIXTH SEALS

The Fifth Seal—Rev. 6:9–11—The Gift of Suffering

With the breaking of the fifth seal we are given insight into what God's people can expect as they seek to live for God's glory among those who despise His name. If the first four seals symbolize life in a fallen world for all the citizens of the earth, then the fifth seal focuses on life for Christians during this same time frame.

Suffering is very much a part of the "abundant life," which Jesus has won for His people, including the suffering of martyrdom. The apostle Paul wrote to believers in Philippi, "For it has been granted to you on behalf of Christ not only to believe on him, but also to suffer for him" (Phil. 1:29). The Greek of this text literally says, "For it has been grace gifted unto you . . . not only to believe . . . but also to suffer." Paul's own life was a testimony to this grace gift of suffering. Even before his conversion God spoke to Ananias of his will for Saul of Tarsus who would become Paul the apostle. "I will show him how much he must suffer for my name" (Acts 9:16).

How many of us consider suffering an expression of the grace of God? We live in a day in which the gospel has been so corrupted that some teach that the only reason Christians suffer is because of a *lack* of faith. What an affront this is to the thousands of Christians who die every year because of the faith! The fifth seal brings encouragement, not just to those Christians suffering in John's day, "because of the word of God and the testimony they had maintained," but also to Christians of *every* generation.

In John's vision he saw a large group of Christians who had already suffered martyrdom. "How long, Sovereign Lord, holy and true, until you judge the inhabitants of the earth and avenge our blood?" (6:10) This longing for justice is not a vindictive attitude or hateful vengeance. Rather, the saints are zealous for the Lord's glory. The world mocks and hates the servants of God and, in so doing, God Himself is held in derision and contempt. This doxological dénouement will occur in full at the second coming of Jesus, and not until then.

God answers His people's cry by calling them to "wait a little longer, until the number of their fellow servants and brothers who were to be killed as they had been was completed" (6:11). What a profoundly encouraging word from our Father! Once again, we see His sovereign grace in action. God is not only in control of the seasons but also of our sufferings, even over the specific number of martyrs!

I race to this Scripture often, not because I view myself as martyr, but because of my own suffering and the sufferings of those in my family and in our church family. As a pastor I am thrust into the midst of all kinds of painful realities and crushing circumstances. The ravages of chronic illnesses; the ripping apart of a family through a loved one's addiction;

that dreaded call from the pathologist confirming a malignancy; the rebellion of a child who once championed the faith; stillborn children and empty wombs—so much sorrow!

There have been many periods in my life, even recent ones, when I have felt overwhelmed with the weight of my own brokenness and pain. More than once I have identified with the apostle Paul when he said, "It would be better by far to depart and be with the Lord." This section in Revelation frees me to express these feelings without guilt and to come to a fresh place of assurance that "Father knows best."

The Sixth Seal—Rev. 6:12–17—God's Impartial Judgment

As the sixth seal is broken, we are given a picture of events that accompany the close of the age and the terror of God's wrath and judgment.

Sin will not go unpunished. A "world gone mad" will not forever prevail. History is heading inexorably towards this great "day of the Lord" when the nations of the world will be judged. Notice the inclusiveness of God's judgment. Kings and princes, generals and foot soldiers, the rich and the poor, every slave and every free man "hid in caves and among the rocks of the mountains" (6:15). No class of people is excluded from the final tribunal. He is the judge of *all* men.

The most important question on that day and this day and any day is "Who can stand?" (6:17). Who will be able to stand up to God's judgment? Each of us will either receive the love of the Lamb or the wrath of the Lamb. We can humble ourselves and receive the full and free benefits of Jesus' death on the cross for our sins or we can despise His love and suffer eternal judgment and the just consequences of our rebellion and sin.

GOD'S ASSURANCES BEFORE THE FINAL SEAL

He Reigns Supremely

Before the breaking of the seventh seal John is given a most encouraging vision, one which expands the meaning and hope of the entire unit of the seven seals (7:1–17). In this magnificent scene we see the hand of God withholding judgment from His people and pouring forth the riches of His grace on them. God's angels, who minister on behalf of "those who will inherit salvation" (Heb. 1:14), are instructed not to "harm the land or the sea or the trees until we put a seal on the foreheads of the servants of our God" (7:3). As the bride of Jesus we are kept secure until and through the day of His judgment. We are "sealed" as a sign of identification—ownership and preciousness to God.

This sealing takes place the very moment someone becomes a Christian (Eph.1:13 ff; Eph. 4:30; 2 Cor. 1:22). John's readers would have been deeply encouraged to know that even as the whole world is in the midst of anarchy and upheaval, and even as they are suffering greatly (many to the point of death), nevertheless, their journey to heaven is secure. Nothing will ever be able to separate the lambs of Christ from the love of the Lamb. Nothing!

He Redeems Abundantly

So just who are these sealed ones? Some have tried to limit the glories of this section to those who have literally died as martyrs. But consider next what John *hears*, "the number of those who were sealed: 144,000 from all the tribes of Israel . . ." (7:4). In verses 4–8 we are given a glimpse of the totality of redeemed humanity, a number that no man can count symbolized by a number whose multiples are 12 times 12 times 1,000. Probably, this is meant to represent the twelve patriarchs of Israel times the twelve apostles of Jesus times one thousand (a number representing magnitude)! Once again we are exposed to this major theme of Revelation: God is indeed faithful to the covenant that He made with Abraham. He has secured the salvation of His people, not just from ethnic Israel but also from all the tribes of "spiritual Israel" (Gal. 6:16; Heb. 11:32, 39ff; 12:22; Gal. 3:29).

In verses 9–10 John goes from hearing of this multitude to actually seeing them. What an international group! Talk about amazing grace! If you are a Christian you are a part of this assembly. These are the true seed of Abraham (Gal. 3:6–9, 16, 28 ff). It is this great company that is able to stand in the very presence of God, now and on the day of judgment. Such confidence comes because "Salvation belongs to our God, / who sits on the throne / and to the Lamb" (7:10) and because "they have washed their robes and made them white in the blood of the Lamb" (Rev. 7:14). God's sovereign grace is the only explanation for such a wonderful redemption! Our God redeems abundantly!

All of heaven joins in the glad and passionate adoration of our Lord who has effected such a salvation (7:11–14). God is worshiped as the One who has loved His people well through the entirety of "tribulation," not just the final outburst of suffering of the people of God. Rather, the totality of pain, suffering, persecution, and sorrow that we know living in this fallen, God-hating world. There was great tribulation for first-century Christians, just as there has been in every century since (Rev. 1:9; Heb. 11:35–38; John 15:18–21; 2 Cor. 4:17; Matt. 5:12).

He Loves Lavishly

Immediately before the opening of the seventh seal John is given one of the most awe-inspiring and inviting pictures of life in heaven for the people of God. There is no section in the book of Revelation that I read more than this one. My own heart returns here time and time again when I am prone to collapse under the weight of all the "stuff" of life, ministry, and the longings of my heart.

Ponder this scene and let it remove from your heart the incomplete and unworthy notions of what heaven is going to be like. With our brothers and sisters from throughout the history of redemption we will be "before the throne of God / and serve him day and night in his temple" (7:15). But consider what is revealed to John next concerning how we will be loved and cared for in our eternal abode. "Never again will they hunger; / never again will they thirst. / The sun will not beat upon them, / nor any scorching heat. / For the Lamb at the center of the throne will be their shepherd; / he will lead them to springs of living water. / And God will wipe away every tear from their eyes" (7:16–17).

This is the fulfillment of *everything* promised in the name, Immanuel. All hunger and thirst is satisfied, forever! And what a paradox: our Lamb has become our Shepherd. Even in heaven Jesus will be ministering to us, loving us, leading us. Glory to God for such tender love and eternal joy! All pain, sadness, and sorrow will be gone.

We will no longer merely "know in part." We will "know fully even as we are fully known." All of God's providences and sovereign dealings will become clear to us. Even the things which we have despised most, the things that have caused us to question the mercy and might of God will be resolved. How I look forward to having complete understanding on why my mom had to die in that car wreck when I was eleven!

I firmly believe (but don't quote me on this!) that for the first thousand years in heaven we are going to hear echoing throughout our Father's house, "Oh, so *that's* what You were doing! Now I see it. Now I understand. Father, Your ways were not always easy but now I see Your glory in all that You did, and I praise You for being so incalculably good and wise."

The Seventh Seal—Rev. 8:1—Silence in Heaven

The seventh and last seal is now opened by Jesus and "there was silence in heaven for about half an hour" (8:1). What could be more appropriate in response to the revelation of the six seals than for there to be a season of stunned silence. "The silence is the silence of awesome expectation."[2] It is silence before the great "day of the Lord" (Zeph. 1:7, 15, 17–18). On the day of judgment God's wrath will silence all who have rejected His grace, for they are without excuse. And on that day, we, the redeemed of the Lord, will be spellbound as we enter into our eternal inheritance.

SALVATION

Revelation 7

FROM THE SONG

One approach to understanding what is taking place in the Apocalypse is to see that by Jesus' coming, the Fall is being undone. A process that began with the first coming is being brought to perfect completion by the second.

In the garden, Adam and Eve experienced separation, not only from God and the garden, but also from each other. The bitterness of their separation is felt in one way or another in every human relationship you and I will ever know. It is also experienced between the nations. We are a separated people. If history teaches us anything, it teaches us this.

This separation of the nations was initiated at Babel when the Lord confused the languages of the people. No longer could they plot against Him en masse, but sadly neither could they praise Him as one people.

At His first coming, Jesus began dismantling all the chaos of this separation. He demonstrated that it was possible for individuals, once separated by sin, to come together through forgiveness. We see the power of this demonstrated in the diversity of the disciples who, though they were educated and uneducated, simple Jews and radical nationalists, loyalists and traitors, were made one and presented as the firstfruits of the undoing. We see the process accelerated further in the ministry of Paul who declares, "There is neither Jew nor Greek, slave nor free, male nor female, for you are all one in Christ Jesus" (Gal. 3:28).

At Pentecost we see further evidence of the reversal of the confusion first experienced at Babel, as the great undoing continues tearing its way through the fallen fabric of history. With great joy I have seen the process firsthand, from China to the U.S. to Northern Ireland, as boundaries disintegrate and as enmity vanishes before the unstoppable power of the undoing—the ongoing Salvation of Jesus Christ.

Sadly, too, I have seen God's own people participate in the wicked work of drawing lines and separating His children on all levels, not realizing whom they were ultimately working against.

But, of course, the central wound of the Fall is the separation experienced between mankind and God Himself. Adam and Eve are driven out of Paradise and the angel with the flaming sword is posted at the gate to keep them and all of their descendants out. Not only are they physically separated, but a dark curtain falls in their hearts and minds as well. Adam foolishly believes he can hide from the omniscient eye of God. In his newfound faithlessness, he thinks he can conceal his nakedness with a clumsy apron of leaves. And from his time until our own we, too, have been about the same foolish business—hiding from the Father who continues to walk through the world seeking us out.

The coming of Jesus also began to undo the great separation between ourselves and God. "If you have seen the Father, you have seen me," He tells His disciples. The great central hope in the heart of God—to walk with us—literally began coming true as Jesus moved about the countryside with His little band in tow.

The conclusion, the final stroke of the undoing, is announced in John's Revelation as the New Jerusalem descends and the loud voice proclaims, "Now the dwelling of God is with men, and He will live with them . . ." (Rev. 21:3). It is the supreme invitation to return to Paradise, which is now the new Paradise of New Jerusalem. But don't forget, it is a promise first made from parched lips to a dying thief by the One who began the great undoing: "Today you will be with me in paradise" (Luke 23:43).

Salvation

Behold a blood-washed multitude
Before the throne of God;
Day and night they serve Him
In the Temple.

As the faithful throng all wave their palms
From every tribe and nation
A heretofore unheard of roar
Joy and jubilation.
Salvation (salvation)
Belongs to our God
To the One who's on the throne.
Salvation (salvation)
Belongs to the Lamb
To our God and to the Lamb alone.

Amen (amen)
Praise and glory
Wisdom, honor, strength, and power
Be to our God for ever and ever
In this eternal, glorious hour.

And they will never thirst again
And neither will they hunger
For the Lamb will be their Shepherd
For the kingdom of this world's become
The kingdom of our Christ.
And God will wipe away the tears
From each and every eye.

CHAPTER SEVEN

REVELATION 8:2–10:11; 11:15–19
THE HOPE OF
COMING JUSTICE

FROM THE WORD

It was just a year ago when the ringing of our phone broke the silence of an early fall evening. "Scotty, this is Carter. You've got to come over here. I think Don is dead. He has apparently been murdered." These words from one of our associate pastors shocked my sensibilities like nothing before. Carter was the first from our pastoral staff to arrive at the home of the director of our Family Ministries, Don Beasley, who had been brutally murdered. Don was the most gentle man I have ever met in my life, not capable of provoking anyone to wrath. As I peered at his crumpled body lying on the floor of the garage I could not help asking, "Lord, where were You in the midst of this great injustice? This makes no sense. How could such a thing happen? Why didn't You intervene, God?"

This is only one of many painful stories I could share from my own experience of the apparent injustice of life in a world over which we are told that God reigns absolutely and sovereignly. No doubt, you could recount many such stories yourself. Yet, we are not alone. One of God's great gifts to us is the reality and honesty of His written Word. He has not edited out the many, many incidents of how His people have been agonizingly vexed and angered at the inequities of life and at the silence and perceived impotence of our God in the face of those who despise His name, reject His authority, and cause great harm to His children. How can evil prevail and even seem to prosper? Is there no justice? Throughout the Scriptures we find God's people asking these questions.

The prophet Jonah struggles with the call to preach to the barbaric Ninevites. He would rather die than live to see God show mercy to the ruthless and arrogant Assyrians who have enjoyed putting their heel on the neck of Israel.

Job and Jeremiah cry out with near curses, wishing they had never been born as they try to figure out the paradoxes and incongruities of God's ways.

In Psalm 73, Asaph, one of the worship leaders in the Jerusalem temple, angrily laments the prosperity of those who have no regard for God and His counsel while he, the man of God, has a painful hunch that the life of faith doesn't really "work."

Habakkuk can't understand how God could use the more godless nation of Babylon to bring the people of God in Judah to repentance. The lamentation, "How long, O Lord?" is chronicled throughout the Scriptures alongside the oftentimes demanding cry, "Why, God?" Our Lord has not hidden the struggle of His people even if He Himself seems to be hiding in the dark recesses of His providence.

Our next section in Revelation, the "Seven Trumpets," speaks to such an ongoing theological conundrum. If the meaning of the seven seals in Revelation 6:1–8:1 can be summarized as: Difficult times mark the "last days" for the people of God, but God protects them, and they have a glorious future, then the meaning of the seven trumpets in Revelation 8:2–11:19 can be summarized as: Difficult times mark the "last days" for the "inhabitants of the earth" (non-believers).

They had better come to their senses and repent during this time of partial judgment and continuing mercy. For justice is coming, both for the people of God and for those who despise the mercy and grace of God.

THE WAIT OF GRACE

The blast of each of the seven trumpets is meant to encourage the hearts of God's people who painfully wonder at God's timetable. Perhaps we would be right to call this aspect of the Christian life the "wait of grace." God promises us sufficient grace as we long for the coming of justice, even as He brings judgment and extends mercy to those who have reviled Him and caused great suffering for His people.

The apostle Paul gives us invaluable insight into this process. To the church of Rome he writes,

> The wrath of God is being revealed from heaven against all the godlessness and wickedness of men who suppress the truth by their wickedness, since what may be known about God is plain to them, because God has made it plain to them. For since the creation of the world God's invisible qualities—his eternal power and divine nature—have been clearly seen, being understood from what has been made, so that men are without excuse. For although they knew God, they neither glorified him as God nor gave thanks to him, but their thinking became futile and their foolish hearts were darkened. Although they claimed to be wise, they became fools and exchanged the glory of the immortal God for images made to look like mortal man and birds and animals and reptiles. (Rom. 1:18–23)

Paul argues that judgment is already being "revealed from heaven" even as final judgment is coming, with the full fury of the holiness and wrath of God. "Or do you show contempt for the riches of his kindness, tolerance and patience, not realizing that God's kindness leads you toward repentance? But because of your stubbornness and your unrepentant heart, you are storing up wrath against yourself for the day of God's wrath, when his righteous judgment will be revealed" (Rom. 2:4–5). All around us God is demonstrating that He is not winking at sin. Judgment now is partial, but it is sure. In this present age God's judgment is part of His redemptive plan to demonstrate His mercy. We Christians are tempted to believe that God is slow to hear our prayers and slow to avenge His glory. Non-believers are tempted to be presumptuous about God's promise to bring judgment against them. They "show contempt for the riches of his kindness, tolerance and patience," which are meant to lead them "toward repentance." Consider how both of these groups are spoken to by the "seven trumpets."

Revelation 8 begins with a vision of "seven angels" who are standing before God and are given seven trumpets— instruments of warning. These angels are likely "archangels," members of the highest order of angels. Another angel appears with a "golden censer." He is given "much incense," which many interpreters see as a symbol of Jesus' prayers for His people. This angel is meant to represent both the importance of our prayers in the outworking of His purposes and the glory of the intercession of Jesus (Heb. 7:25; 9:24; Rom. 8:34; John 17:9, 20 ff). In response to the prayers of the saints we see the censer now filled with elements of judgment and destruction. God hears the cries of our hearts and the longing of our souls. His judgment is sure, present, and to come!

So we see a natural division between the first four trumpets and the last three. As with the seven seals, the first four trumpets largely show the effects of God's present judgment on the inanimate world; the last three demonstrate

His judgment against mankind in particular. As we read through this section, noticeable parallels can be seen between these judgments and those that God visited on the Egyptians during the time of the Exodus (Ex. 7–11). The greater exodus from sin and death effected by King Jesus is now being accompanied by God's judgments in history as well.

The First Trumpet Blast: The Earth Is Stricken— The Environment Is Affected

As the first angel sounded his trumpet, "hail and fire mixed with blood" was "hurled down upon the earth" (8:7). A third of the earth, trees, and green grass were burned. "Hail and fire" remind us of Exodus 7:14–9:22. "A third" is meant to convey the idea that these judgments are severe but not total. It is still the hour of mercy. This trumpet represents any kind of destruction which at any time damages the earth. What we call natural or environmental disasters or tragedies are to be seen as God getting our attention. He whispers in our pleasures and shouts in our suffering. The recent wildfires in California and the hurricanes along the eastern coast can be understood as a part of God's present judgment.

The Second Trumpet Blast: The Sea Is Stricken— Commerce Is Affected

The second trumpet heralds the throwing into the sea of "something like a huge mountain, all ablaze" (8:8). Once again we find this judgment affecting a third of the sea, of living creatures in the sea, and of the ships. The original recipients of this letter would have naturally thought of the Mediterranean. And in their own time they had witnessed both the eruption of Mt. Vesuvius (A.D. 79) and the sacking of Jerusalem in A.D. 70. Did the prayers of God's people figure into the destruction of Pompeii and Herculaneum? We cannot say for sure, but let us realize that this section of Scripture does teach us that God uses the prayers of His people to accomplish His sovereign purposes. Such a fact is staggering to ponder. Through this trumpet God also affects the commerce of the world as there was great dependence upon maritime welfare for economic welfare. Sometimes the only thing that seemingly is capable of redirecting the minds and hearts of non-believers towards heaven is for the money supply to be shaken and threatened. When I was teaching this section to the members of our church family someone asked if God's periodic "thumping" of the Dow Jones average is an example of this trumpet. I could not agree more.

The Third Trumpet Blast: The Rivers Are Stricken—Natural Resources Are Affected

With the blowing of the third trumpet, a third of the rivers and springs of water turned bitter as a "great star, blazing like a torch, fell from the sky" (8:10–11). The star was named "Wormwood." That which is meant to give life actually brings sickness and death "to many." John's Jewish readers would have remembered a similar account of God's judgment brought to bear in Jeremiah's day.

What man is wise enough to understand this? Who has been instructed by the LORD and can explain it? Why has the land been ruined and laid waste like a desert that no one can cross? The LORD said, "It is because they have forsaken my law, which I set before them; they have not obeyed me or followed my law. Instead, they have followed the stubbornness of their hearts; they have followed the Baals, as their fathers taught them." Therefore, this is what the LORD Almighty, the God of Israel, says: "See, I will make this people eat bitter food and drink poisoned water." (Jer. 9:12–15)

God can eliminate the power of natural water to slake our thirst so that a deeper thirst might be quickened, one which can only be slaked by the living water of the gospel.

The Fourth Trumpet Blast: The Sky Is Stricken— Man's Vision Is Affected

As the fourth angel blows his horn of warning, the means by which men see are substantively affected. A "third of the sun was struck, a third of the moon, and a third of the stars, so that a third of them turned dark. A third of the day was without light, and also a third of the night" (8:12). How is this judgment being realized in our world? Eclipses, smog, sandstorms, nuclear cloud-cover? We cannot say for sure. "The supernatural events of the Bible are concerned not with 'How?' but with 'Who?' and 'Why?' Trumpet four again points us back to the book of Exodus, where the importance of the plagues which struck Egypt was precisely that men could not understand how they happened and had to admit that God was at work (Ex. 8:7, 18 ff)."[1] John opens his own gospel with the tragic editorial comment on the hearts of mankind when he says, "In him was life, and that life was the light of men. The light shines in the darkness, but the darkness has not understood it" (John 1:4–5). God will intensify the darkness so as to create a longing for the true Light.

After the blowing of the fourth trumpet, an eagle, which is often a symbol of judgment as it feeds on the carnage and remains of those under God's discipline (Matt. 24:28, KJV; Luke 17:37, KJV; Job 39:27–30), appears in John's vision, calling out three woes which prepare us for the intensification of judgment of the next three trumpets (8:13). The remaining three trumpet blasts are directed against the stubborn and rebellious who continue to refuse to listen to the warnings and wooings of the living God.

The Fifth Trumpet: The Locusts from the Pit— Torment (Rev. 9:1–11)

Whereas the first four trumpets speak of God's judgment in the world in which men live, the next three speak of judgment on the men of the world. Satan emerges on the scene as an instrument of God's judgment. He is the "star" that fell from heaven (Luke 10:18). His power is "given" to him. God is sovereign over all things, including the delegated authority and power of all demonic forces and their captain, Satan.

From the "Abyss" emerges an ugly army of locusts (cf. Ex. 10:12–15). These locusts are used to torment all of those on the earth who persist in refusing the grace and mercy of God (those who have not already been sealed by the Spirit of God). This army of hell is given a commission to do their destructive work for "five months," perhaps an allusion to the normal life span of certain locusts or a reference to the 150 days the water stayed upon the earth at the time of the Flood (Gen. 7:24). In any case, it is important to see that their time and terror are in the hand of God.

Their appearance is probably derived from Joel 1–2, in which we find clear reference to locusts as a symbol of God's judgment. The "king" of these warlike insects is Satan himself, the "destroyer" who is also heading for his own destruction. I agree with Michael Wilcock who believes that "whenever unbelievers suffer in this way, all the many-shaped ills which torment them, and which even kindly death will not come to relieve—chronic hardships, diseases, enmities, insecurities—

these ills are the locusts of Trumpet Five, marshaled and led by the angel of the Abyss . . ."[2]

The Sixth Trumpet: Angels at the Euphrates— Destruction (Rev. 9:12–21)

With the blowing of this trumpet the judgment of God gets even more intense. Angels are released to kill "a third of mankind," a significant minority. Along with them an incredible army of horsemen ride forth, perhaps a great "demonic army," who, along with the angels, are tools of God's sovereign and deserved judgment of the world. In the ancient world, the Euphrates was believed to be the boundary between the East and the West, the eastern boundary established by God for the descendants of Abraham (Gen. 15:18). Through much of biblical history the main threat of destruction came from the region of the Euphrates and the Tigris—Assyria and Babylon, for example.

This sixth trumpet, like the rest, announces a strong warning of God's wrath against sin in response to the prayers of God's people that evil should not go on forever and that it should not be unpunished. How is such judgment being revealed in our world? In every way imaginable. Through bad health, terrorist acts, war, "accidents" of all varieties. Tragically, as with trumpet five, we see pain but no repentance. What an indictment against the foolish hearts of men. Nothing is left but final judgment, signified in the blowing of the seventh trumpet.

An Intervening Vision: The Magnificent Angel and the Little Opened Scroll (Rev. 10:1–11:14)

Before the last trumpet is blown an incredibly large and splendid angel appears with legs that straddle the earth and the sea. Many believe him to represent the worldwide spread of the gospel and the scroll to be the Word of God, "with the message of salvation in Christ on every page."[3] The only escape on judgment day is to have believed the gospel. As the gigantic angel shouted, John heard "the voices of the seven thunders." But even as the apostle Paul was not permitted to write down or reveal what he saw in the "third heaven," so John is instructed to "seal up what the seven thunders have said and do not write it down" (10:4). We simply cannot know some things.

Next, the angel announces that God will delay His judgment no longer. The day of mercy is about to give way to the day of justice. John is told to eat the scroll in the angel's hand, a reminder of the prophet Ezekiel's experience of eating the bittersweet Word of God (Ezek. 3:1–3). The gospel and the Christian life contain things pleasant and things difficult, both are part of God's good and glorious plan.

The Seventh Trumpet: The Glory of the Church— (Rev. 11:15–19)

With the blowing of the seventh trumpet we are introduced to the end of the ages as we know them. This is the eschaton, the final day, the Day of the Lord! This vision is the fulfillment of the great promise made to the prophet Isaiah concerning the expansion of the kingdom of God, a kingdom whose increase and whose peace will know no end! And King Jesus, the greater David, will reign for ever and ever. Every time I sing this great passage set to music in Handel's *Messiah* I am simply overwrought. Every longing in my soul is ignited at the anticipation of this awesome and glorious day. Martin Luther said that there were only two days on his calendar, this day and *that* Day. Because *that* Day is coming, *this* day can be lived with hope and patience.

I offer this final word of caution and encouragement as I

conclude this chapter. The topic of the judgment of God has given rise to some very confused thinking and destructive practices by God's people. We must be very careful not to make the same mistake that the friends of Job made. Their error was to assume that any difficult circumstance in the life of a believer, or nonbeliever, could be traced to a particular sin. Thus, they continued to persist in grilling Job on the details of his life and the obvious lack of obedience to God that led to his encounter with so many tragedies. Such mathematical moralism has much more in common with pagan philosophy and Oriental karma than it does with a biblical worldview. At the end of the book of Job, it is they rather than Job who receive the divine rebuke for misspeaking about God and His ways.

Likewise, we find Jesus confronting this same formula-based mentality in the Gospels. In John 9 we read of an encounter that Jesus has with a man who was blind from birth. "His disciples asked him, 'Rabbi, who sinned, this man or his parents, that he was born blind?' 'Neither this man nor his parents sinned,' said Jesus, 'but this happened so that the work of God might be displayed in his life'" (vs. 2–3). The same false assumption had been made by the disciples of Jesus that had been made by the friends of Job: Bad things do not happen to good people. And yet here we find Jesus introducing a rather novel concept: Difficult things often happen to all kinds of people that God might display His glory. In the end, all things ultimately concern the glory of God. All things.

In Luke 13, another incident is recorded in which Jesus contradicts the prevailing attitude towards calamities in the lives of individuals.

Now there were some present at that time who told Jesus about the Galileans whose blood Pilate had mixed with their sacrifices. Jesus answered, "Do you think that these Galileans were worse sinners than all the other Galileans because they suffered in this way? I tell you, no! But unless you repent, you too will all perish. Or those eighteen who died when the tower in Siloam fell on them—do you think they were more guilty than all the others living in Jerusalem? I tell you, no! But unless you repent, you too will all perish." (Luke 13:1–5)

The point that Jesus is making is obvious. Let none of us assume that we are less deserving of the judgment of God than anyone else. For we all fall short of His glory. And let none of us assume that we are in a position to determine the specifics of the sovereign administration of God's blessings and judgments. The rain falls on the just and the unjust even as the storm and waves come to the houses of those who have built on both a bad and good foundation.

How does all of this relate to the blowing of the Seven Trumpets of Revelation and our hope of coming justice? What attitudes should we seek to cultivate?

As hardships, heartaches, and reversals occur around us, let us hear "trumpets blowing," but let us resist the temptation to label every difficult event as an obvious expression of God's judgment. That is neither our prerogative nor our calling. The secret things belong to the Lord. The mysteries of providence are just that, mysteries.

Let the hard things that happen to us as the people of God remind us that we are not home yet. Even though we are perfectly forgiven, we do not yet live in a perfect world. The consequences of sin and fallenness are all around us.

As we witness "divine intrusions" into the world around us, may the compassion of God move us to pray for the conversion of those touched by God rocking His world. While it is right to long for the day of justice it is never right to nurture a heart of self-righteousness and vengeance. This is a theme that we cannot hear too often. (Thus, I repeat it in this book more than once!) As we ponder the sobering reality of the incremental growth of God's judgment throughout the world, let us become more and more humble and compassionate as we never lose sight of the mercy that our Father has lavished upon us in His Son. We who were without mercy have received mercy. Let us extend it to others.

CHAPTER EIGHT

REVELATION 11:1–14
THE HOPE OF MEANINGFUL
WITNESS AND IMPACT

FROM THE WORD

Reid Christy, one of my good buddies growing up from elementary through high school years, lived on a big farm with horses only a ten-minute walk from my home on Oakwood Lane. We all loved to hang out there, play backyard football, and just do "stuff" that guys like to do. His mom made the best turkey breast and homemade bread sandwiches (which I coveted any day Reid brought one to school for his lunch) in the universe. There always seemed to be a smile for me at the Christy's home and table. It was one of those places where I really felt the welcoming heart of God even before I came to know Him as my true shelter.

But one of the most profound memories that I have of the Christy farm and family was the time they installed the first "bomb shelter" I had ever seen. It was during the Cuban Missile crisis when President Kennedy took such a strong stand against the threat of Premier Khrushchev's maddening quest to have Russia swallow the world. How can I ever forget his threats, theatrics, and tirades at the United Nations, banging the heel of his shoe on the desk top as he arrogantly planned for the day in which Communism would consume the whole world? Never has a cold war seemed so ready to thaw out and lead us to the first all-out nuclear war, maybe that dreaded World War III that we little guys heard so much about from our dads and other veterans.

In the atmosphere of real fear and great concern the "bomb shelter" business thrived! I remember feeling a certain amount of ambivalence when the Christys installed their little underground steel house. "Will there be room for me in here? I've always been invited over to spend the night. Can I still spend the night if Russia invades North Carolina?" These real concerns of "wars and rumors of war" were never very far from our hearts in those days, and for good reasons. This was no idle threat. Communism was laying waste to much of my then-known world. Gradually, however, this season gave way to another, less ominous one, and my friends whose families had bought into the "bomb shelter" mentality began to convert their shelters into musty storage units or underground attics.

This was not the last time I experienced the "bomb shelter" mentality, however. While the first one was political and generated by the threat of communism, the second one was spiritual and generated by the threat of the "Antichrist." A lot more fear than faith was generated in my heart, and in many of my late '60s Christian counterparts, by those who were constantly searching the newspapers and newsreels in order to interpret the last book of the Bible. Oh, the bad exegeses and sensationalism that were being forced on us by those apocalyptic prophecy mongers whose popularity was only exceeded by the growth of their seminars and book sales!

The net effect of those who made their living by feeding and growing our phobias and suspicions was the retreating of Christians from the culture into little ecclesiastical bomb shelters. Christian communes were being planned and established in many parts of America. The buying of common properties, stockpiling of food stuffs, and multiple warnings against owning or receiving anything with the number 666 on it were profuse. Guessing the identity of the Antichrist became a growing and popular sport among those who were becoming less and less engaged with the world into which we have been commissioned as witnesses and kingdom representatives until King Jesus returns. It really makes me both mad and sad as I look back over those days, for this is just the opposite effect that the book of Revelation is meant to have.

As we turn our attention to Revelation 11:1–14, we are introduced to the section that John records for us just before the blowing of the seventh trumpet. It is similar to the intervening vision which he received just before the breaking of the seventh seal in its intent to bring great encouragement, hope, and courage. In Revelation 7:1–17 we saw the sealing of the 144,000 and the white-robed multitude emerging triumphant after a lifestyle of great persecution, suffering, and tribulation during the whole interadvent period (the whole age between the first and second comings of Christ). In Revelation 11:1–14 we are given a vision of the Lord's two witnesses who emerge triumphant after a life of faithful witness, and yet who suffer a brief and apparent defeat.

After John has the vision of the great angel straddling the whole earth with the "bittersweet" gospel in his hand, he is next told to "measure the temple of God and the altar, and count the worshipers there" (11:1). This measuring is similar to that which the prophet Ezekiel was commissioned to do in Ezekiel 40–42, but with a very significant difference. In the New Testament we find that the temple of God actually becomes the people of God (1 Cor. 3:16–17; 1 Pet. 2:5; Eph. 2:20–22). John's vision does not concern the temple in

Jerusalem made of stone, which was destroyed in A.D. 70. Rather, his focus is on the temple made of "living stones," the people of God from every race, tribe, and tongue, who are becoming a dwelling place for the Lord by His Spirit. As Philip Hughes has commented, "The measuring commanded here is an indication to us of the ordered perfection of all that God purposes and performs, as the Creator and Restorer of the universe. Its measuring may be taken to mean that God is in control of all that happens to his servants, they are well-known in number and name to God."[1]

John is next told, "But exclude the outer court; do not measure it, because it has been given to the Gentiles. They will trample on the holy city for 42 months" (11:2). This brings us to one of the most debated details in the whole book of Revelation. What are we to make of this forty-two-month period of time? It occurs several times in Revelation as "1,260 days" and "time and times and a half a time."

The background to this numeric symbol is found in Daniel 7:25; 9:24–27; 12:7. The most popular interpretations of this three-and-a-half-year period have been these: 1) the second half of the seven-year Great Tribulation in which Antichrist rules; 2) a conventional symbol for a limited period of unrestrained wickedness; and 3) the whole inter-advent period. During this period the Gentiles "trample the holy city," that is, the people of God are persecuted. When John received this vision, Jerusalem had already been destroyed. We must look to the following verses for a more complete understanding of the meaning of this part of the vision.

In Revelation 11:3–14 we meet the "two witnesses" who are raised up and empowered by God for faithful and effective ministry during this whole persecution-filled, 1,260-day period. They are identified by means of Old Testament imagery. Perhaps we are to be reminded of Moses and Elijah who appeared with Jesus on the Mount of Transfiguration (Mark 9:4) and who had "power to shut up the sky so that it will not rain during the time they are prophesying; and they have power to turn the waters into blood and to strike the earth with every kind of plague as often as they want" (11:6).

Perhaps the "two-ness" is not a limited number but rather a symbol of the trustworthiness of their witness (John 8:17 ff; Deut. 19:15; Luke 10:1; Acts 1:8). Certainly, the two "olive trees" and "two lampstands" should remind of us the spirit-filled church called and empowered to preach the gospel in light of all kinds of opposition and persecution, including that of martyrdom (Ps. 52:8; Zech. 4; Rom. 11; Rev. 1–2). For in the Old Testament the olive tree was often used as a symbol of Israel, and, as we have already seen in Revelation, the lampstand signifies the church.

As the two witnesses continue their effective ministry among the nations, John records a fatal attack from "the beast that comes up from the Abyss" (11:7), but only after "they have finished their testimony." Satan's attack does not and cannot alter that which our Father has purposed. The gospel *is* running through the nations. There *will be* men and women from every people group populating heaven. The kingdom of the world *will become* the kingdom of our Lord and of His Christ, and *He will reign* for ever and ever!

The attack of the beast on the witnesses leads to their *death* and a brief three-and-a-half-day period of gloating, celebrating, and gift-giving among the peoples of the "great city," here referred to as "Sodom and Egypt," which stand for hardened idolatry and rebellion. In the following chapters of Revelation, Rome (also referred to as "Babylon") is identified as the world in rebellion against God and His people (2 Cor. 4:7–9; Jer. 5:11, 14; John 15:18–21).

What seemed to be the death of the witness of the church

actually gives rise to her resurrection and glory! "But after the three and a half days a breath of life from God entered them, and they stood on their feet, and terror struck those who saw them" (11:11). Should we not think of this three-and-a-half-day apparent triumph as a type of the three days that Jesus spent in apparent defeat after His crucifixion? The beast's victory is hollow! (Ezek. 37:10; Acts 7:54–56; 1 Cor. 15:20 ff; 1 Thess. 4:16, 17; 2 Cor. 4:4). God's enemies are startled, humbled, and overwhelmed when He vindicates His servants. How much more so will be the case at the second coming of Jesus when every knee will bow and every tongue confess that Jesus is Lord to the glory of God the Father (Phil. 2:1–11)!

Let us now try to imagine how this vision of the two witnesses would have affected the hearts of John's original audience. Of what practical and timely importance would this image have been to persecuted Christians in the first century if the forty-two months or 1,260 days was a reference to something that would happen only thousands of years after their deaths? On the other hand, if the three-and-a-half-year period is indeed a reference to the whole interadvent period, the whole age between the two comings of Christ, then we can see great relevance and encouragement not only for Christians of the first century, but also for Christians of every century.

As the people of God we are known, numbered, loved, and protected against all ultimate harm and loss. We are not to develop a "bomb shelter" mentality in the face of great opposition and persecution. Our calling never has been to retreat into little Christian cocoons, communes, or communities of navel-gazing fear, self-protection, and survival. For John's readers in Asia Minor there is great encouragement. They are not to fear Rome's worst assaults. Even though there will be times and places in which it seems that the church has been silenced and defeated—if not destroyed—the demise is only brief and apparent. For the blood of the martyrs has always proven to be the seed of the church. Our God is the God of resurrection. Even though the enemies of God have a seasonal laugh at the temporary demise of the witness of the gospel, He who sits on His throne in heaven laughs eternally and the loudest (Ps. 2).

What about the church of every age? What hope, comfort, and courage do we derive from this vision? Our calling is not to waste time trying to run from Visa cards with 666 on them. We aren't to debate among ourselves if the birthmark on Gorbachev's head means he's the Antichrist. We are, by proclamation and by presence, to preach and demonstrate the gospel of Jesus Christ among the nations until Jesus comes back. We, the church, are the two witnesses. We are empowered by God Himself. He is the Lord of both miracle and persecution, of both gospel advancements and apparent gospel setbacks. Our calling is not to be successful, but to be faithful.

Perhaps we American Christians need this life-giving rebuke more than any other segment of the Body of Christ. Am I guilty of exaggerating or being unfair to suggest that we have done more to perpetuate the "bomb shelter" mentality of Christianity than any other people group? Most evangelical pollsters indicate that between 30 and 40 percent of Americans claim to be "born-again Christians." Shouldn't we expect our culture to be significantly affected by the kingdom of God with this many Christians living here? J. I. Packer, a gracious theologian from Great Britain whose lecture I was privileged to hear, described our American Christian spirituality as about "three thousand miles wide and two inches deep"? Are we more veneer than substance?

What are we afraid of? This is our Father's world. None

will ultimately thwart His ways. No, we are not to be naive about life in "Sodom and Egypt." In fact, the next chapters of Revelation have much to teach us about how to live wisely in the midst of antichristian ideology. And yet, God gives us insight about the "real world" so that we can serve Him with confidence and hope as we seek to demonstrate the radical implications of the gospel in our own context of "Babylon."

We are all missionaries! As witnesses we are to go into every nation of the world and every sphere of life. A part of our repentance is going to require that we recognize and discard some of our non-biblical thoughts and paradigms about what it means to be a witness and to be involved in ministry.

First of all, let's repent of our pragmatism. The driving question of ministry is not "What works?" The missionary to Afghanistan who may see one convert in ten years is not to be considered either a failure or ineffective. God alone is the One who faithfully applies the saving benefits of Jesus Christ to the lost. It is up to the Lord of the harvest how this mystery is played out. Our calling is simply to "declare His glory among the nations." He alone can raise the dead, and He does!

On the other hand we must be careful not to label some missionary or pastor or gifted layperson a "superstar" in the Kingdom in terms of great observable fruit. As the apostle Paul asked the Corinthians rather rhetorically, "What do you have that you did not receive? And if you did receive it, why do you boast as though you did not?" (1 Cor. 4:7). God gives talents, gifts, calling, and fruit as He sees fit. One plants, another waters, another harvests, but it is God who causes the increase. As Francis Schaeffer has said, "There are no little places and no little people"[2] in the economy of eternity. This is a theme we continue to emphasize in our church family.

Second, we need to repent of bifurcating the ministry of

the Word and the ministry of good deeds. God's grace needs to be communicated by proclamation and by presence. Saint Francis once charged his followers to "go and preach the gospel, and use words if you must." Now I readily admit the ease with which such a statement can be both misunderstood and misapplied. But I am equally aware of how we evangelicals tend to do a far better job of preaching at people than coming alongside of them as conduits of the mercy of our God. Unfortunately, we tend to think that unless a full-blown presentation of the gospel has been given then we have failed in our calling as witnesses. May God enable us to beautify the truth of the gospel as we manifest the grace of the gospel.

I have learned much about the power and importance of ministries of mercy through a remarkable young woman on our staff named Paige Overton. Paige was raised by parents who have both been afforded many creature comforts that the world can offer. Yet the true riches of the gospel are what have seized their hearts and consciences. Paige tells me that extending the love, compassion, and mercy of Jesus is quite natural for her because she has seen her parents live with such freedom and focus. She cannot remember a time when there were not foster children in her home. Unselfish living has been modeled for her since day one. She is a rich woman indeed.

Paige directs a ministry through our church called Franklin Community Ministries. The heartbeat of this outreach is the conviction that the gospel is not just about getting people into heaven (as important as that is!), but it is also about getting heaven into people. Jesus is a reconciler, a healer, and a transformer of life and culture. Paige, and those who labor in love with her, live to see the power of the gospel confront and change the divisions among us affected by sin.

Our church is located in a city that has a history of racial strife and religious pride. Franklin Community Ministries is being used by our Lord to invade many of the real battle-fields in our community that exist because of the fallenness of man, economic inequity, educational stratification, ecclesiastical division, and a Southern "caste system." These and other issues are on a collision course with the mercy of Jesus through Paige and her many co-workers. May our Lord increase their number. Much glory is being given to our God, and that is the primary goal of any ministry. Perhaps it would be far easier to simply put gospel tracts under the windshield wiper blades of all the cars in all of the parking lots of Franklin, but what in Revelation 11:1–14 indicates that a life of witnessing is to be easy?

Third, we need to be careful not to limit the concept of "ministry" to what we commonly refer to as "spiritual activities." For instance, why is a summer mission trip taken by a businessman or woman considered "ministry" but his or her vocation—what he or she does the rest of the time—is simply referred to as a job? During the Reformation, Calvin, Luther, and others were mightily used by our God to help Christians reclaim the doctrine of "vocation." By this concept they have helped Christians for many generations understand that *every* sphere of life is to reflect the glory and grace of God. All enterprises are not to be graded, distinguished, or valued in terms of the evangelistic opportunities they afford.

God is honored when we do all things to His glory. This is the essence of what it means to bear "witness" to His name. As image bearers of God we should want to reflect both His genius as a Creator and His mercy as a Redeemer. If we preach, let us do so with precision and with passion. Do not distort the gospel and do not dishonor our Lord by not preparing your sermon and your heart. And if you are plumber, then plumb to the glory of God. Putting a little fish sign or a cross on one of the pipes you install will not make the job you performed "Christian." Indeed, if you did a poor job please do not put any such sign on your work! God is more honored by a non-Christian doing a good job than when we, His people, do slipshod or halfhearted work.

This whole issue plays out in our church family in a *big* way in our music. Of the four thousand or so members who call Christ Community home, a significant percentage of our adult population have vocations in the music industry, both the *Christian* and *secular* music industries. The emphasis on the preceding words is intentional because it reflects how much we are in need of a biblical worldview of the arts, sciences, entertainment, literature, economics, politics, and education. What is *Christian* music? Music is not deserving of the appellation "Christian" just because it may have religious lyrics, a recognizable religious melody, or because it is performed by a Christian. Some of the most un-Christian music I have ever heard is sold in Christian bookstores. Poor theology, bad music, and greedy motives are not the components of art that has been created to bear witness to the glory of God among the nations!

To suggest that music, or any art form, is "Christian" only to the extent that it is directly about some biblical theme or only if it serves the purposes of evangelism or religious training is an equally spurious notion. One of the first heresies that invaded and affected the first-century church was gnosticism, a Greek worldview that distinguishes all of reality between "spirit" and "matter." The realm of spirit is to be prized while the realm of the material, the created work, is to be denigrated if not despised. Such an unbiblical worldview has led Christians almost totally to disregard the revelation of God as the sovereign Creator and eternal sustainer of all things. We have compartmentalized life into categories that cannot be justified by the Scriptures. The net effect is that the gospel, and Christians, are removed from the public square and from primary contexts in our culture. Christian faith is marginalized and trivialized. What is worse, God is robbed of the glory due His name.

In our church family, I get far more excited about hearing and seeing how Christians are serving the purposes of God faithfully in the marketplace than I do when I hear of one more bored and boring believer going overseas to reproduce their superficial spirituality among the naive and impressionable. I have greater joy when a musician in our fellowship hones his or her craft well enough to earn a first chair position in the Nashville Symphony or wins an audition to be the lead guitarist for a popular country music group than when I hear of another musician signing to a Christian music label. Call me prejudiced if you must. I pray that I am not cynical. I know that I have a great passion to see Christians get out of the evangelical ghetto into this mainstream of our culture where we are commissioned to be salt and light by what we say and what we do.

Until Jesus returns we are to move courageously and expectantly into the world and into the culture where our Lord has placed us. For a day is coming when the earth will be filled with the knowledge of the glory of the Lord as the waters cover the sea. In light of this hope, let us live well and love well in every sphere of life . . . all to the glory of God.

CHAPTER NINE

REVELATION 12–14
THE HOPE OF
GOD'S PERSPECTIVE

FROM THE WORD

No book in the Old Testament has meant more to me, theologically and practically, than the book of Job. It's not that I would dare to compare my experience of suffering with Job's. For even though I have known some great pain and heartache in my forty-six years, when I ponder God's providential orderings for Job, my whining and complaining stop real fast. It is not primarily as a sufferer that I have found great import and impact from this part of the Old Testament canon relegated to the books called "wisdom literature."

Why, then, is Job so important to me? In many ways it represents the slow-but-steady work God has been effecting in my heart as His Spirit and Word have brought me to a more mature understanding of the nature and mystery of the Christian life. In essence, God continues to use Job to show me the huge difference between my perspective and His perspective. And in so doing He has utterly convinced me of the necessity, freedom, and joy of an ongoing surrender to His vantage point and purposes. He has also taught me (I wish I could say once and for all) the tragedy and misery that come from leaning on my own understanding in an attempt to comprehend the drama of life.

It's just at this point where the book of Job and the book of Revelation converge. Both are books of crisis and conflict and the ensuing struggle to make sense of what it means to be God's people in the crucible and vortex of history. And both represent many voices asserting the right to be the interpreter of all things. God, man, misguided "friends," one's painful heart, Satan, the state, culture, false prophets—who has the ear of our inner man? To whom have we given the sacred right to interpret the circumstances and exigencies of our pilgrimage towards the New Jerusalem? Perspective is often the only difference between paralyzing fear and liberating faith in the lives of the people of God. Both Job and John were reduced to soul-staggering silence and worship of Him who does all things well.

In Revelation 12–14 we are invited to view what few earth dwellers could ever hope to see. God pushes back the curtains of human history and lets us peer backstage to know what is really going on behind the scenes, behind all the fury of the human drama that has been under way ever since Adam and Eve sinned against our Father in the Garden of Eden and was intensified with the birth of Jesus, the only Savior of the world. We are not only introduced to the main characters but are also given a copy of the whole story line, including the wondrous climax of a script that God alone could write and produce! Insight into these things is not meant to "ruin a night at the theater" by our knowing the end of the play before the first curtain rises. Rather, God gives us this holy privilege and gift that we might be filled with hope as we assume our role in His sovereign plans and purposes.

It's important at this point to highlight what John saw after the seventh trumpet of warning and judgment is blown. After the saints are rewarded and the destroyers are destroyed (11:18), John writes, "Then God's temple in heaven was opened, and within his temple was seen the ark of his covenant. And there came flashes of lightning, rumblings, peals of thunder, an earthquake and a great hailstorm" (11:19). This living snapshot of the "ark of the covenant" bridges us from one of John's several recorded vignettes of the end of history into a whole new section of his letter. Let's remember that John's visions are recorded for us in the order he saw and heard these things, not necessarily in the order in which things happen. The significance of this transitional image is pointed out by Michael Wilcock: "Of the ark, no more need be said here than that it is the symbol of God's covenant, or agreement, to rescue his people from their enemies; and the lightnings, voices, thunders, earthquake, and hail are often used in Scripture as signs that he is present and active."[1] At every point in the letter God reminds us of His mercy and His might. What follows in Revelation 12:1–15:4 is the telling of the story of God's active covenant to His people to deliver them safely to heaven.

The Main Characters in the Drama of History (Rev. 12:1–6)

"A great and wondrous sign appeared in heaven: a woman clothed with the sun, with the moon under her feet and a crown of twelve stars on her head. She was pregnant and cried out in pain as she was about to give birth" (12:1–2). This woman clearly represents the people of God, "the human stock from whom Jesus came" (represented at the time of Jesus' birth by Mary, the mother of our Lord). Our lives matter to God and our place in history is no small place.

"Then another sign appeared in heaven: an enormous red dragon with seven heads and ten horns and seven crowns on his heads. His tail swept a third of the stars out of the sky and flung them to the earth. The dragon stood in front of the woman who was about to give birth, so that he might devour her child the moment it was born" (12:3–4). Here John introduces us to the devil, Satan, our chief adversary. His seven heads represent his authority, the crowns his "royalty," and the ten horns his very great strength. "The dragon positions himself to seize and destroy the woman's child. Nothing, indeed, is more urgent for him than to devour the Son who is coming in the world to destroy the devil and his works (1 John 3:8; Heb. 2:14)."[2] The dragon *hates* the Son. This hatred was behind Herod's cowardly act of murdering so many young male children at the time of Jesus' birth (Matt. 2:16 ff).

"She gave birth to a son, a male child, who will rule all the nations with an iron scepter. And her child was snatched up to God and to his throne. The woman fled into the desert to a place prepared for her by God, where she might be taken care of for 1,260 days" (12:5–6). This "male child" is none other than the Lord Jesus, the Messiah, who was taken up to heaven after His death and resurrection and who will one day return to "rule the nations" (Ps. 2; Isa. 9:6 ff; Phil. 2:6–11). These three—Jesus, Satan, and Mary, or the people of God—are the main players in the drama of history, and with shorthand efficiency John sets the scenario for the unfolding of the whole interadvent drama. Just as Israel was in the wilderness for forty-two years en route to the Promised Land, so the church will be in the desert for forty-two months (1,260 days). The entire period between the two comings of Christ will be full of conflict in an evil world. But God will protect and provide for His people and safeguard them against all ultimate harm.

War in Heaven: The Dragon Is Cast Out

In Revelation 12:7–16 we are next given priceless insight into the nature of spiritual warfare. This vision would have been timely and invaluable to John's readers, just as it has proven to be both enlightening and encouraging for God's people of every generation. Satan's hatred of God and His purposes is set forth in terms of a "war in heaven." His defeat by the Lord Jesus, the "son," the "male child," is presented in graphic apocalyptic language. The "dragon" and his allies are simply "not strong enough" to prevail against the host of heaven. Satan, who seeks to "lead the whole world astray," was "hurled down" by King Jesus and he, along with his "angels" (demons) is en route to "eternal fire" (Luke 10:17 ff; John 12:31; 16:11, 33; Matt. 25:41: Rev. 20:10).

There is already "much rejoicing in heaven" over this defeat. Jesus came to destroy the works of the devil, and He succeeded! God's people in the first century and in every century overcome him and his ploys by the word of the Lamb and by the word of their testimony (Phil. 4:13; 2 Cor. 12:9 ff; Rom. 8:31–37). The gospel of God's all-consuming grace frees them and us not to love our lives "so much as to shrink from death." Let us, therefore, "rejoice," but let us also be wise. For Satan, knowing he is defeated and knowing "that his time is short" is going down swinging. His massive dragon tail is swinging wildly and destructively for he is "filled with fury."

The Dragon Persecutes the Woman and Her Offspring

Having failed to destroy the Son, Satan spends the rest of his days seeking to destroy the sons and daughters of the living God. How predictable it is to see that Satan's hatred of

Jesus is now turned toward those whom Jesus loves, His bride. Satan knows that his time is limited, and our destiny is most glorious; therefore, he will do anything in his power to make life miserable for us now. This is the essence of spiritual warfare: The hatred of Jesus by our vanquished adversary marshaled against us, the followers of the Lamb.

Jesus told us to expect trouble in this world, great trouble. But as we "hope in the LORD" we are borne up and along as on "eagles' wings" (Isa. 40:31; Ex. 19:4). Until the end Satan will spew a river of evil at us, but God will protect and provide for us. He will never leave or forsake us. How different this perspective is from much of what I see among Christians in our American culture. On one hand I see so much doubt, fear, suspicion, sensationalism, and uncertainty, one wonders if the news ever reached us that Jesus has already won the victory over Satan. That first great promise of the gospel in Genesis 3:15 has been realized. Satan is a real but a defeated foe. We overcome him now by the blood of the Lamb, by the once-finished work of the Lord Jesus upon His cross. We overcome him by the word of our testimony. When the gospel is believed and lived out every day until we are in heaven. We prevail because Jesus has prevailed. This truth is meant to sink deep into our souls.

But as many Christians err on the side of unbelief and fear so many others err on the side of naïveté and presumption. To affirm that Satan is our defeated foe is not to say that he is no longer a mighty adversary. He has been dethroned, not annihilated; conquered, not eradicated. A helpful way of thinking of Satan's defeat and the limitations of his authority over believers is to envision him on death row, held on an unbreakable chain. The life of grace and wisdom requires that we do not venture within the length of the chain which binds our enemy; we also learn to accept God's sovereign purposes in giving the forces of evil certain limited power to serve His ultimate purposes in the world.

In the words of the apostle Paul we need to be wise "in order that Satan might not outwit us. For we are not unaware of his schemes" (2 Cor. 2:11). Much of the remainder of Revelation is written unto this very end: that we know the schemes and end of Satan and his host of allies. In Revelation 13 we are introduced to the dragon's two great allies, "the beast from the sea" and "the beast from the earth." Together they form a counterfeit trinity, a "trinity of evil."

The Beast from the Sea

This ghastly beast with multiple horns, heads, and crowns has its corollary in the four great beasts that Daniel saw coming up out of the sea (Dan. 7). Four successive world powers living in great hostility to the people of God proved to be the fulfillment of Daniel's vision. In a similar way many scholars have suggested that John's vision of the sea beast is to be understood as political and societal persecution for the church in every generation. Certainly for John's original readers, the Roman Empire would be the embodiment of this evil, this Antichrist. Philip Hughes comments, "This beast should be taken as denoting the activity of the devil throughout the history of this age by the instrumentality of human movements and organizations rather than a single individual." It is "the spirit of antichristianity manifested, as we have said, through human agencies during the whole course of the Christian era, though perhaps achieving its final and fiercest force under the leadership of a malevolent personage in the ultimate climax of history (1 John 2:18; 1 John 4:3)."[3] Michael Wilcock adds, "So when we are shown a beast whose power is not that of wealth or of influence, but that of government ('diadems' and a 'throne'), who combines all the powers of Daniel 7, we see in him the principles of power politics: in a word, the state."[4]

The goal of this beast is obvious: to seize the adoration, attention, and allegiance that alone belong to the Lord Jesus. "He opened his mouth to blaspheme God, and to slander his name and his dwelling place and those who live in heaven" (13:6). Beginning with Julius Caesar, Roman emperors were deified, mostly after they had died. But, as already mentioned, Emperor Domitian required that people address him as "our lord and god." The beast's deceit is such as to even counterfeit the death and resurrection of Jesus through "a fatal wound, but the fatal wound had been healed" (13:3). His persecution of Christians serves the purpose of seeking to gain the worship of "all whose names have not been written in the book of life belonging to the Lamb . . ." (13:8). Therefore as followers of the Lamb we are called to "patient endurance and faithfulness."

The Beast from the Earth

The next member of the trinity of evil to be introduced is the beast from the earth. His lamblike facade is a superficial cover for his dragonlike reality. His intent is to promote the worship of the sea beast through "great and miraculous signs, even causing fire to come down from heaven to earth in full view of men" (13:13). "The first beast comes up out of the sea. The second arises from the land. The first is Satan's hand. The second is the devil's mind. The first represents the persecuting power of Satan operating in and through the nations of this world and their governments. The second symbolizes false religions and philosophies of the world."[5] John will later identify this second beast as the "false prophet" (Rev. 16:13; 19:20). "It symbolizes false philosophy in whichever form these appear throughout the entire dispensation. It symbolizes all false prophets in every era of this dispensation. They come to you disguised as sheep, but inwardly they are ravenous wolves"[6] (Matt. 7:15).

The Mark of the Beast

Now we come to one of the most hotly debated details in the entire book of Revelation. "He [the earth beast] also forced everyone, small and great, rich and poor, free and slave, to receive a mark on his right hand or on his forehead, so that no one could buy or sell unless he had the mark, which is the name of the beast or the number of his name. This calls for wisdom. If anyone has insight, let him calculate the number of the beast, for it is man's number. His number is 666" (13:16–18).

Who is the personification of evil symbolized by the number 666? By using the practice of "gematria," assigning a numeric significance to letters of either the Greek or Hebrew alphabet, these are among the many who have qualified for this great dishonor: Caesar, Nero, Martin Luther, Caligula, Domitian, various popes, Protestant Reformers, Oliver Cromwell, and John Wesley. Take your pick!

But perhaps we have been asking the wrong question. Maybe we should ask, "*What* does this number signify?" for John simply says that the number stands for the beast. Philip Hughes helps us here: "The one clue that St. John gives is that the number of the beast, 666, is the 'number of man.' The number six has understandably been regarded as a symbol of man, in that it falls short of seven, which is the divine number. On this basis the threefold six may be understood as indicative of a human or humanistic trinity, that is to say a counterfeit of the divine Trinity, with all the pretensions to supreme power and authority that such a counterfeit implies. It may perhaps be inferred from the context that this pseudo-trinity is that of Satan (the dragon), plus antichrist (the first beast), plus the false prophet (the second beast), who are united in the one diabolical objective, namely, to dethrone the Creator and to enthrone the creature and to substitute the image of the beast for the image of God in man."[7]

Therefore, 666 shows up in every generation and every place throughout the whole interadvent period. What is this mark and when does the marking take place? Do we need to be concerned about Visa cards, driver's licenses, social security numbers, and the like which contain this number? Does it not make more sense to see that John is presenting the counterfeit trinity's equivalent "seal" to that of God's? As God has sealed His people as a sign of ownership, so the beast of the earth seals those who are his.

The consequences for the people of God are obvious. To confess that Jesus is Lord and that Caesar is not is to find it oftentimes very difficult to "buy and sell," that is, to carry on an interrupted life as a part a corrupt and anti-Christian world and culture. Manifestations of this kind of persecution were happening in first-century Rome for believers who refused to burn incense to Caesar. And in every generation since the cost of following Jesus, rather than the dragon and his minions, has been documented by tears, blood, loss, privation, and even death.

During my entire Christian life, 99 percent of the discussions that I have heard about the "mark of the beast" have given rise to speculation, doubt, and fear. But consider what next fills John's vision and heart after God has given him insight into this diabolical trinity.

The Lamb and the 144,000

"Then I looked, and there before me was the Lamb, standing on Mount Zion, and with him 144,000 who had his name and his Father's name written on their foreheads"

(14:1). Rather than being left to dread Satan and to fear his ways John is led to worship God and delight in His ways! In Revelation 14:1–5 we are given a vision of Jesus standing as victor on Mt. Zion, the place of redemption, not on Mt. Sinai, the place of law. He is the victor over the dragon, the sea beast, and the earth beast. All of his people share in His victory. (Let us remember that this 144,000 represents the totality of the people of God.) They are signed, sealed, and delivered safely to the Father by the triumphant Lamb.

Worship breaks out in heaven, which sounded to John like "the roar of rushing waters and like a loud peal of thunder" (14:2). This loud, passionate, and joyful worship is the people of God singing the new song accompanied by the string players of heaven. They are described as those who follow the Lamb and who "were purchased from among men and offered as firstfruits to God and the Lamb" (14:4). Only in heaven will we fully understand and believe that "salvation is of the Lord." God bought us, He redeemed us by the blood of the Lamb, plus nothing!

The Three Angels

John is next given a vision of three angels "flying in midair" (14:6–13). These angels represent a very God-centered view of the main issues of life between the comings of Christ. Spiritual warfare is not the story of the cosmic conflict between two equal adversaries battling it out in the heavenlies and on the earth. Spiritual warfare is about the advancement of the gospel among the nations of the world in the midst of real, but ultimately futile, opposition. Thus, the first angel speaks of grace and impending judgment (14:6–7). Until the last hour the gospel will be preached among the nations, but God's patience is not without limits. Those who despise His mercy will know His wrath.

The second angel forewarns of "Babylon's fall" (14:8). All godless systems and philosophies and ideologies of the "world" and the Antichrist are doomed. God's truth and Kingdom will prevail over all things, everything the dragon and all of his allies can muster. Lastly, the third angel highlights the eternal consequences of one's worship (14:9–13). To worship the beast is to be guaranteed eternal torment. To "die in the Lord" is to be guaranteed eternal rest. This is the main issue in life and in death: to whom or what have you given your worship? True or false worship is at the heart of what we call spiritual warfare.

As Professor Bruce Metzger puts it, "Men and women are so constituted as to worship some absolute power, and if they do not worship the true and real Power behind the universe, they will construct a god for themselves and give allegiance to that. In the last analysis, it is always a choice between the power that operates through inflicting suffering, that is, the power of the beast, and the power that operates through accepting suffering, namely, the power of the Lamb."[8]

Grapes of Wrath: The Final Reaping

After the third angel flies on, John is given a vision (14:14–20), similar to that which Daniel received in Daniel 7:13. The "Son of Man" of Daniel's vision is Jesus, coming in glory as the judge of all men (Matt. 13:24–30, 36–43).

Where is the entire history of the world heading? Toward this day when King Jesus will bring forth the harvest of His judgment on the living and the dead when the "time to reap is come." God alone knows the hour of this appointed day. In John's vision there are two aspects of Jesus' reaping: the reaping of the wheat, which represents Christians, and the reaping of the tares, those who have rejected Jesus and His atoning death (Matt. 9:37; Luke 10:2; John 4:36–38; Mark 4:26–29).

What a tragic scene this is for those who refuse the free grace of our God through Jesus. Rather than be taken to the bosom of God by His love they will be under His feet in judgment. Such is the insanity of sin and such is the judgment of God upon all who do not love His Son. We will either cleave to the One who was trampled under God's judgment "outside the city" for us (Heb. 13:12), or we, ourselves, will be trampled under His feet "outside the city," justly, because of our sin (Isa. 63:1–6; Joel 3:13). Which will you have?

THE DRAGON

Revelation 12

FROM THE SONG

You never see the personality of the white witch more clearly than in the scene in *The Lion, the Witch and the Wardrobe*"[9] where she stands before Aslan, the great lion, and accuses Edmund of his treachery. She is telling the truth of course. The boy has betrayed his brothers and sisters and even Aslan. The witch reveals that his sin has given her power over, and even possession of, the frightened little boy—a power that it seems even Aslan can do nothing about.

But of course there is the deep magic from before the dawn of time that she knows nothing about. She understands sacrificing others but cannot grasp the notion of someone sacrificing themselves for another. This becomes her undoing and Edmund's salvation.

Though we see her riding through the endless Narnian winter in her sleigh, though we witness her cruelty as she turns good animals into stone, we never see her more clearly than when she stands before the great lion as the accuser.

You and I know, too, that to broadcast the sinful failings of others is to gain a sort of power over them. It is just as true with our own accusing gossip as with the white witch or the evil one. To accuse someone is to gain power over him. To become an accuser is to participate in the work of the evil one.

Any military person will tell you that before you engage an enemy you first seek to understand his character, his flaws and weaknesses, as well as his strengths. To defeat another you must see him as clearly as you can.

We never see the character of Satan more clearly than when he stands before the throne of God and accuses the brethren (Zech. 3:1). He believes that by his accusations he is gaining power over us and God. What he does not understand, and indeed will never understand, is that the One before whom he stands and hurls his accusations has forgiven and forgotten these sins. He has already given Himself for their salvation. Like the great stone table in Narnia, the power has been broken by the Lion who is the Lamb.

The Dragon

A vile enormous dragon
With heads and horns and crowns
And a tail that swept
The stars from heaven
And cruelly cast them down,
He lurked before the woman

Who was about to bear her Son,
The One who'll come to rule the nations
With a rod of iron.

Now has our salvation
The power and kingdom of God,
For the dragon is defeated
By the word and the blood of the Lamb.

Behold, a war in heaven
Reflected here on earth,
And Michael and his angels
Fought for all their worth
That wicked, ancient serpent
Who leads the world astray,
The accuser of the brethren
Was beaten from the fray.

Rejoice then, oh you heavens,
Woe to the earth and sea;
For he is filled with fury
'Cause he knows his time is brief.

CHAPTER TEN

REVELATION 15–18
THE HOPE OF
VICTORY OVER EVIL

FROM THE WORD

The very first cliché I remember hearing about the book of Revelation was "I read the end of the book and we win!" To a competition-minded, sports-loving young Christian of the late '60s, that sounded great. It reminded me of the feeling I got when it was time to play neighborhood baseball or football and I knew Tommy Adcock, the kid whose collision with puberty took place way before it did with the rest of us, was on my team. Not only did we envy his firstfruits of mustache hair but his testosterone level enabled him to excel in any sport he played. He was "the man."

As a young believer I guess I thought of Jesus as a big Tommy Adcock and the Christian life as the "mother of all Super Bowls." Because Jesus was on *my* team, I was destined to win! Spiking footballs in the end zone of life and passing out confident high fives of victory to teammates in the presence of vanquished opponents pretty well defined my spiritual attitude. Unfortunately, some of the theologies of the Christian life that were floating around in those days actually supported and fed such a perspective. I thank our heavenly Father for His unlimited patience and forbearance toward such a naive and self-centered son like me!

But as I have continued to study God's Word, my perspective on my place in the economy of eternity has changed radically. A theological Copernican revolution of great proportion and implications has occurred: I have discovered that the Son does not revolve around me, I revolve around the Son! He is the center of all things. I finally understand the wisdom of the framers of the Westminster Confession of Faith who affirmed that the chief end of man is "to glorify God and to enjoy Him forever."

Joshua learned this lesson as he was leading the people of God into the Promised Land. After their covenant with God was reaffirmed at Gilgal, through the young men being circumcised and the whole nation celebrating the Passover, Joshua prepared to take God's people toward Jericho (Josh. 5:9–15). As he came close to the city "he looked up and saw a man standing in front of him with a drawn sword in his hand." Joshua asked this imposing figure, "Are you for us or for our enemies?" In essence, "Whose team are you on?" His answer to Joshua's inquiry is classic, "Neither," he replied, "but as commander of the army of the LORD I have now come." Then Joshua fell facedown to the ground in reverence and asked him, "What message does my Lord have for his servant?" The commander of the Lord's army replied, "Take off your sandals, for the place where you are standing is holy." And Joshua did so.

The angel of the Lord, whom many Old Testament scholars identify as the Lord Jesus in His pre-incarnate form, makes it real clear that He is not merely the star player on a team. He is the Lord! The battles ahead for the people of God, as they move into Canaan, are His battles. The Promised Land is to be the launching pad for His glory among the nations. As we have seen throughout the book of

Revelation, God loves His people with a passion and delight that most of us have only begun to realize. But God's love is the means by which we are freed from a life of self-preoccupation to a life of being preoccupied with our Lord and His purposes. "For Christ's love compels us, because we are convinced that one died for all, and therefore all died. And he died for all, that those who live should no longer live for themselves but for him who died for them and was raised again" (2 Cor. 5:14–15).

Such a heart is reflected in John the Baptist when he said of Jesus, "He must become greater; I must become less" (John 3:30). We also see this spirit in the apostle Paul when he affirmed, "For to me, to live is Christ and to die is gain" (Phil. 1:21); and "I consider my life worth nothing to me, if only I may finish the race and complete the task the Lord Jesus has given me—the task of testifying to the gospel of God's grace" (Acts 20:24). Already in Revelation we have witnessed this freedom and focus in the martyrs who "loved not their lives unto death."

These who have followed the Lamb before us clearly understood that Jesus does not join our team to help us win in life. He didn't come to baptize our self-interests. Jesus teaches us to pray, "Your kingdom come, your will be done" (Matt. 6:10). Through the gospel we are grafted into His heart and made partakers of His purposes and triumph! Perhaps a better way to summarize the later chapters of Revelation, then, would be, "I read the end of the book and Jesus wins and will reign forever!"

This is the perspective that is both reflected in and cultivated by the sobering section of Revelation to which we now come. Chapters 15 through 18 record the pouring forth of the wrath of God on those who choose to worship the beast rather than the Lamb. This vision of John also includes the final defeat of all the forces of evil allied against the people of God, which is personified by the great harlot, Babylon.

God's people of the first century must have been deeply encouraged by such a promise. Rome would not ultimately prevail over the church, even though the evidence seemed to indicate the opposite. And God's people of every generation have been filled with this same hope. No nation, no power, no tyrant, no evil will ultimately prevail against the Lord and His plans for His people. Jesus has won. Jesus will win!

Seven Angels with Seven Plagues: The Saints Rejoice

Revelation 15 begins with John seeing another great and marvelous sign: seven angels with the seven last plagues—last, because with them God's wrath is about to be executed in its fullness and finality. This vision is preparation for the final outpouring of God's judgment upon a world that has rejected His Son. Whereas the seven trumpets represent God's painful warnings for those who refuse His grace, the seven plagues, or "bowls of wrath," represent the promise of punishment. As history progresses, this judgment intensifies and will culminate in the final battle between Jesus and the great dragon, between the church and the world.

Realizing that the time is near for God to vindicate fully His honor, the redeemed people of God rejoice. They have no fear of the coming wrath of God, for they have already passed from judgment to life in Christ. They "sang the song of Moses the servant of God and the song of the Lamb" (Ex. 15:1 ff; Deut. 18:15, 18; John 6:14; 7:40; Acts 3:22). As God has graciously delivered His people in the past from the evil and power of Pharaoh, so He delivers them through one who is greater than Moses—Jesus, the King of the ages.

"Great and marvelous are your deeds,
  Lord God Almighty.
Just and true are you ways,
  King of the ages.
Who will not fear you, O Lord,
  and bring glory to your name?
For you alone are holy.
All nations will come
  and worship before you,
for your righteous acts have been revealed." (15:3–4)

Again we see that the worship of God is the theme that ties the entire book of Revelation together. At every turn we find God's people directing their hearts to Him who alone is worthy. The utter God-centeredness of their adoration is telling.

Bruce Metzger says, "One of the most striking features of this song of the triumphant martyrs is the absence of any mention of their own victory and their own achievement. From beginning to end the whole song is a lyrical outburst celebrating the greatness of God."[1] The greatest satisfaction, the deepest worship, and the highest praise is enjoyed by those whose main interest and joy in life and in death is the glory of God.

As John's vision continues he sees further preparation for the revelation of God's righteous judgment. "Then one of the four living creatures gave to the seven angels seven golden bowls filled with the wrath of God, who lives for ever and ever. And the temple was filled with smoke from the glory of God and from his power, and no one could enter the temple until the seven plagues of the seven angels were completed" (15:7–8). The prayers of God's people for the vindication of His honor are answered as the bowls full of the incense of their intercession (Rev. 5:8; 8:3) now give way to the bowls full of God's wrath.

Holy Wrath or Irrational Rage?

The concept of the wrath of God is, understandably, a very difficult one for many of us to accept, both intellectually and emotionally. This is especially the case in a humanistic culture in which utilitarian views of God prevail. Without a knowledge and understanding of God's holiness, we tend to think of Him as a benign and benevolent grandfather who is somewhat under obligation to do good. After all, we reason, "God is love and, therefore, He owes me."

On the other hand, we tend to think of ourselves, and mankind in general, not as sinners who desperately fall short of the glory of God, but rather as victims for whom life has not been fair and who need to be pitied and understood more than we need to be forgiven and changed. Instead of crying out to God for mercy, we tend to demand compliance with our inalienable rights to be appreciated and taken care of. Unfortunately, this attitude has crept from the world into the church.

We, like John, and Isaiah before him (Isa. 6:1 ff), need to see God's holiness and majesty afresh. For only then will His grace and mercy move us to great humility and gratitude for the great salvation He has given us so freely. The cross of Jesus is robbed of its import and glory when we minimize both our guilt and the fullness of God's wrath that fell on Jesus when He took upon Himself the judgment we deserve. Until our hearts and tongues are silenced by God's holy otherness and moral perfection, we will not be able to understand and accept the revelation of His wrath that is to come in full upon the world. This wrath is not the irrational rage of an agitated pagan deity. Rather, it is the righteous and pure indignation of God towards all evil and His resolute action in punishing sin.

THE OUTPOURING OF THE SEVEN LAST BOWLS OF WRATH

It was a rather sobering time in our Bible study at Christ Community as we approached this topic. There were many good questions raised and we all agreed how limited our perception of the perfection and purity of our God is. We lamented this reality and asked God to have mercy on us as we sought to understand more of His righteous character and ways. Far from simply "licking our chops" about the coming Day of the Lord when the "bad guys are going to get it," we learned more about our call to holiness and the importance of gratitude for Jesus, the "Rock of ages," who rescues us from the coming wrath.

The First Bowl: The Earth Is Stricken—Rev. 16:1–2

"The first angel went and poured out his bowl on the land, and ugly and painful sores broke out on the people who had the mark of the beast and worshiped his image" (16:2; Ex. 9:9–11).

Using the imagery of the plagues visited on Egypt during the Exodus, John demonstrates the increase and growing intensity of God's judgment upon those who worship the beast instead of the Lamb.

When the health of man is disturbed, his attention is often piqued. As we get closer to the second coming of Jesus, we should not be surprised to witness God's finger touching that which our culture often turns into a primary idol—physical health. Medical science and wonder drugs are no deterrent against God's purposes. Those who pretend immortality must learn of their mortality.

One of the members of our Bible study asked if I felt that sexually transmitted diseases, especially AIDS, could be considered an example of this "bowl." My answer was a qualified "Yes." Certainly, such a tragic illness fits the paradigm of this judgment, but I am not sure that such a question is at all the point of the text.

Nowhere in Revelation is it suggested that we are called to identify and label horrible events, disasters, and illnesses as "obvious" expressions of God's judgment. Let us not say more about such matters than the Scriptures do. For instance, we all know by now that AIDS is not exclusively transmitted through sinful sexual behavior. To suggest that everyone who has AIDS is under the wrath of God is unfair. But either way, our calling is to the compassionate demonstration of the truth of the gospel: to those who both love our Lord and to those who despise Him; to those who are HIV-positive and those who are negative. We are not called to self-righteously pronounce judgment but to weep over our own sins and call others to find shelter in Jesus against the coming Day of final judgment.

The Second Bowl: The Sea Is Stricken—Rev. 16:3

"The second angel poured out his bowl on the sea, and it turned into blood like that of a dead man, and every living thing in the sea died" (16:3).

Now it is not just the sea, but life in the sea that is affected. Here we see God intensifying judgment against man's commerce, livelihood, and supply (Ex. 7:20–21).

My son loves to fish. He is a master angler, and our Lord has put within him a godly respect for the environment. Every time he hears of the diminishing numbers of game fish or the poisoning of wildlife, his heart hurts. I think of him when I read these verses. Scott knows the source of all life, but there are many who simply take all things for granted. But God will not be mocked. He will shake every foundation, He will disturb every arena of pretense and presumption as His wrath is revealed from heaven.

For those in John's day, the provision of the sea was the source of life. God's judgment falls on those places where we tend to place our confidence without reference to Him. Woe to those who think that there is a stock portfolio thick enough to withstand the decrees of God. Natural resources cannot replace supernatural resources. This will become more and more evident as we race toward the end of history.

The Third Bowl: The Rivers Are Stricken— Rev. 16:4–7

With the outpouring of this bowl the "rivers and springs of water . . . became blood" (vs. 4). As the Euphrates River fed and nourished ancient Babylon, so Rome, the contemporary Babylon of John's day, was dependent on her waters. But all presumption will be arrested. Every aspect of God's creation is affected by His judgment. There is no place to hide. The only way to run from God is to run to God!

This bowl represents the vindication of God's name on behalf of His people in a similar way to what we saw when the fifth seal was broken (Rev. 6:9 ff). The angel cries out, "You are just in these judgments, / you who are and who were, the Holy One, / because you have so judged; / for they have shed the blood of your saints and prophets, and you have given them blood to drink as they deserve" (16:5–6).

And the people of God at the altar in heaven respond: "Yes, Lord God Almighty, / true and just are your judgments" (16:7).

Christians of every generation need to be reminded to always leave room for God to take His own vengeance. It is His to repay! (Rom. 12:17, 19). It is not wrong for us to look forward to this day, but it is terribly wrong to long for this day with a heart of cynicism, self-righteousness, and retaliation.

The Fourth Bowl: The Sky Is Stricken—Rev. 16:8–9

Literally, the heat of God's judgment is turned up as this bowl releases the sun to "scorch people with fire." The darkness of the sun brought about by the blowing of the fourth trumpet will not bring men to repentance; neither will its searing heat. What an accurate and tragic picture of just how hardened the human heart can be. The destructive power of the sun simply caused the impenitent to curse "the name of God, who had control over these plagues, but they refused to repent and glorify him" (16:9).

As we continue to reflect on these bowls of judgment the progression from wooing the foolish to woe-ing their foolishness becomes clearly evident. John is not being redundant, he is simply demonstrating the ongoing theme and intensification of the judgment of God being visited in the world.

Giving us a helpful summary of the relationship between the seals, the trumpets, and the bowls, Michael Wilcock says, "Again and again trouble will sweep the world (the Seals); whenever suffering is caused, God warns that it cannot be caused with impunity (the Trumpets); whenever His warnings go unheeded, He will in the end punish the wrongdoers (the Bowls)."[2]

The Fifth Bowl: Torment—The Beast's Kingdom Is Darkened—Rev. 16:10–11

"The fifth angel poured out his bowl on the throne of the beast, and his kingdom was plunged into darkness. Men gnawed their tongues in agony and cursed the God of heaven because of their pains and their sores, but they refused to repent of what they had done" (16:10–11).

Now John sees the entire human system thrown into confusion and anarchy (Dan. 4:17, 25, 32; 7:12). God's throne, not that of the beast, is in ultimate control. As this bowl is emptied on the world, we observe the absolute insanity of sin in the unwillingness of those who worship the beast to receive the love of the Lamb.

As I write these words, I have to stop and thank God for rescuing me from my own insanity. To think of the years that I was more attracted to the kingdom of the beast than to that of the Lamb. "Oh, to grace how great a debtor, daily, I'm constrained to be." I deserve this coming judgment every bit as much as those who will receive its full force and horror on that great Day.

The Sixth Bowl: Destruction—The Final Battle—Rev. 16:12–16

With the pouring forth of the sixth bowl, we are led to the brink of the final battle of the war, which has been fought between the seed of the woman and the seed of the serpent ever since God put enmity between the two (Gen. 3:15). John refers to this final conflict as "the battle on the great day of God Almighty" (16:14). It is fought in "the place that in Hebrew is called Armageddon" (16:16).

No one knows for certain what "Armageddon" means and this is the only place where the name even occurs. There is not even a consensus among biblical scholars concerning its correct spelling. Many suggest that it is a reference to Megiddo, a place where battles were fought from time to time in Israel's history.

John's vision of this last chapter in the war of the ages depicts each member of the "trinity of evil" spewing out evil spirits that look like frogs. These spirits have power to perform "miraculous signs, and they go out to the kings of the whole world, to gather them for the battle" (16:14).

Jesus prepared his disciples for this demonic subterfuge with these words, "False Christs and false prophets will appear and perform signs and miracles to deceive—if that were possible, the elect" (Mark 13:22). Likewise the apostle Paul warned that the "lawless one" would come "in accordance with the work of Satan displayed in all kinds of counterfeit miracles, signs and wonders, and in every sort of evil that deceives those who are perishing. They perish because they refused to love the truth and so be saved." (2 Thess. 2:9–10).

These foul, lying spirits mobilize "the kings of the whole world" in a final mutiny against God, His purposes, and His people. The whole war and this final battle were written about in Psalm 2:1–6, in which David muses:

> Why do the nations rage
>   and the peoples plot in vain?
> The kings of the earth take their stand
>   and the rulers gather together
> against the LORD
>   and against his Anointed One.
> "Let us break their chains," they say,
>   "and throw off their fetters."
> The One enthroned in heaven laughs;
>   the Lord scoffs at them.
> Then he rebukes them in his anger
>   and terrifies them in his wrath, saying,
> "I have installed my King
>   on Zion, my holy hill."

Such is the perspective and attitude that we should take towards Armageddon, and even towards the whole of spiritual warfare. The most important issue before us is not *when* and *where* this conflict will occur but rather the fact that *it will occur* and *it will accomplish God's intended purpose*. The outcome of this battle and the total war is certain. Because Jesus has triumphed, Jesus will triumph!

It is a real battle with real casualties. But even in dying we live! Jesus has conquered death for us. The last enemy to be defeated is Death itself. Nations and kings of the earth be warned. You are no threat to the living God. He has already installed His King in Zion. He is Jesus, the King of the Ages! "Kiss the Son" while there is still time.

The Seventh Bowl: The End of the World— Rev. 16:17–21

When the seventh angel "poured out his bowl into the air" a loud voice was heard from the temple saying, "It is done!" (16:17). History as we know it is brought to a conclusion with this announcement. This is the terrible "Day of the Lord" (Heb. 12:26 ff; Matt. 24:21, 29; Hag. 2:6).

"As always, however, God is the refuge and strength of His people, who therefore are without fear, 'though the earth should change and the mountains should shake in the heart of the sea' (Ps. 46:1; Joel 3:16). They are assured, indeed, that they will receive a 'kingdom that cannot be shaken' (Heb. 12:28)—the kingdom that will break in pieces and bring to an end all enemy kingdoms, while it itself is indestructible and stands forever" (Dan. 2:44).[3] May we *never* forget that the wrath which falls upon non-believers in the final judgment is the wrath that fell upon Jesus on His cross. He died in *our* place. He has suffered in full that which we fully deserve. Let our hearts be sobered. Let our hearts be glad.

Judgment Upon the Allies of the Dragon— Rev. 17–18

In Revelation 15–16 we witnessed the coming judgment upon those who have repudiated God's saving grace and who have refused to bow the knee to the true King. In Revelation 17–18 we are given a vision of the judgment and end of the characters and conduits of evil which have perpetuated Satan's foolish and fatal attempt to usurp God's glory.

In an age of "computer-speak," it's as though God now clicks on the icon of "Babylon," a representation to the Israelites of wickedness and persecution and to John and his readers, a symbol of Rome with all of her "seductive luxury and vice" and anti-Christian bias. In so doing, God gives us in full what He has already given us in part: the promise and hope of the final victory over Satan's kingdom won by Jesus upon His cross. The destruction of Babylon does not follow the events of the seventh bowl of wrath. Rather it is a central aspect of the cataclysmic end of history. The end of all things is highlighted here to bring both wisdom and encouragement to the hearts of God's people in every age who live in the midst of the evil tyranny of the dragon and his allies.

Babylon: The Seductive Whore Destined for Disaster—Rev. 17:1–6

Says one of the seven angels to John, "Come, I will show you the punishment of the great prostitute, who sits on many waters. With her the kings of the earth committed adultery and the inhabitants of the earth were intoxicated with the wine of her adulteries" (17:1–2). Judgment has already been pronounced on "Babylon" in Revelation 16:19, but Christians are warned by this Scripture not to take her allurement and temptations lightly. Though this whore's end is most definitely assured, she will seek to seduce and destroy until the last day. Babylon represents what the New Testament more often refers to as "the world"; not the physical creation, but the fallen ideology and worldview of those who continually seek to live in open antagonism and indifference to the Tri-une God of the Bible.

The Beast and the Whore: Collaboration of Evil—Rev. 17:7–14

The angel gives John invaluable insight into the nature of the dragon's network of evil. The "unhappy hooker" rides upon the back of the beast "drunk with the blood of the saints" (17:6). Though these perpetrators of evil and persecution are indeed enjoying a season of apparent victory, their defeat and doom are certain. In these verses we are given a description of the rise, demise, and rejuvenation of evil in our world.

One of the great mysteries of providence is the way our sovereign heavenly Father uses even evil to serve His ultimate purposes. He controls the ebb and flow of all things. The cooperation of all evil forces, civil and supernatural, will make a final and furious stand against the Lamb, "but the Lamb will overcome them because he is Lord of lords and King of kings—and with him will be his called, chosen and faithful followers" (17:14). What a glorious paradox: the beast is overcome by the Lamb!

The Self-Destruction of Evil—Rev. 17:15–18

"The beast and the ten horns you saw will hate the pros-titute. They will bring her to ruin and leave her naked; they will eat her flesh and burn her with fire. For God has put it into their hearts to accomplish his purpose . . ." (17:16–17). What a surprise. Satan's kingdom will ultimately be divided against itself and fall! (Matt. 12:26). Evil will ultimately col-lapse beneath the tonnage of its own rancor and rebellion.

What comfort this must have been to Christians living under the persecution of insidious Roman emperors like Nero, who according to the pagan historian Tacitus of the first century wrote, "a vast multitude of Christians were not only put to death, but put to death with insult. They were either clothed in the skins of wild beasts and then exposed in the arena to the attacks of half-famished dogs, or else dipped in tar and put on crosses to be set on fire, and when the daylight failed, to be burned as lights by night" (Annals XV, 44). Even though the "woman," this pernicious whore, is permitted to rule "over the kings of earth," her reign of evil is about to come to an end.

The Great Fall of Babylon the Great—Rev. 18:1–24

It is interesting to note that the longest song recorded in Revelation concerns the overthrow of Babylon. Many Bible scholars agree that this dirge is a New Testament version of the many songs of doom sung by the Old Testament prophets against the nations who waged war on Israel. John's writing reflects his familiarity with the prophecies of Isaiah and Jeremiah marshaled against Babylon (Isa. 13, 21, 47; Jer. 50, 51) and those of Ezekiel directed against Tyre (Ezek. 26, 27).

A most glorious angel whose splendor illumines the whole earth arrives in John's vision to announce with a shout: "Fallen! Fallen is Babylon the Great!" The day of God's vengeance has come for "God has remembered her crimes." She will be paid back double for all the destruction wrought by her abominations. "Give her as much torture and grief as the glory and luxury she gave herself." God promises His church concerning this harlot, "In one day her plagues will overtake her: death mourning and famine. She will be consumed by fire, for mighty is the Lord God who judges her." Hope is stirred within the church while lament is generated among the kings, merchants, shipowners, and sailors of the earth.

There will be weeping and wailing among those who have profited from the whore's prostitution and adulteries. These will not be tears of repentance but selfish tears of depression over the forfeiture of worldly position, power, and possessions. Jesus told a parable of just such a man in Luke 12. He is referred to as the "rich fool." Such is the man or woman who, deluded by Babylon's false promises, "stores up things for himself but is not rich toward God" (Luke 12:21). To such a person God says, "You fool! This very night your life will be demanded from you" (Luke 12:20). With the prosecution of the prostitute also comes the judgment of all who have loved her ways.

A "mighty angel" throws a huge boulder into the sea to symbolize the violence with which Babylon will be thrown down, once and for all (18:21). Life will never be the same in Vanity Fair. Her pleasures and magic spells were for a season, but now the season is up. Evil will cease to exist. Hallelujah!

THE CITY OF DOOM

Revelation 18

FROM THE SONG

Like people, cities have different personalities. It might be the power hungriness of a Washington or a Beijing, the vanity of a Nashville or Hollywood, the greed of a Las Vegas or New York, or the bitterness of a Belfast or Los Angeles. Certain cities, like people, have their certain sins, and they attract citizens with similar personalities.

In Revelation, two cities are mentioned: Babylon, the whore, and Jerusalem, the bride. The first is the seat of the great cult of consumption. The second is the place of the Holy One. One is destined for destruction; the other to become the beloved of God forever. One attracts people bent on believing the lie that everything can be bought for a price; the other lovingly draws those who hope that the best anyone can hope for is the free gift of God.

Amid all the poems and hymn fragments contained in Revelation, this is by far the longest. We might think that the more celebrative fragments, like the "Song of the Lamb," should be the longest. Surprisingly, it is only two verses long while the song of the fall of Babylon extends well over twenty verses! Detail after detail is given concerning her downfall. Sights, sounds, and smells engage our imaginations as we "see" this great city (a code word for Rome) utterly destroyed and forgotten forever. One can almost feel the heat of the consuming fire and hear the tumultuous crash as the city comes down.

Her downfall should be understood as a prelude to the great "hallelujah!" which occurs in the very next verse. The wealth of detail is meant to paint a picture of everything the Kingdom of God has fought against from the beginning and over which it has now been victorious. The magnitude of her destruction is in inverse proportion to the rejoicing of the saints and must be experienced before the full force of the "hallelujah!" can be felt.

Yes, certain cities have certain sins, but they also have certain destinies. The ultimate question is not the identity of the city but the direction in which it allows itself to be drawn. Is it for greed, the hunger for power or fame, or even despair that some cities choose to be known? Or will they pattern themselves after the new Jerusalem, the city of peace, the spotless bride? The Word says, "Choose . . . this day . . ." (Jos. 24:15). Which will you choose?

The City of Doom

Come out of her, my people,
And never go back again.

For all her vulgar vanities
Have been heaped up
As high as heaven.

The nations drank
Her maddening wine
Now God's remembered all her crimes,
And she'll be paid back double
For all that she has done.
Fallen, fallen, fallen
Is Babylon,
Fallen, fallen, fallen
Is the City of Doom.
The queen of every dark desire,
Consumed by famine, plague, and fire;
Fallen is Babylon
Fallen is the City of Doom.

Never will the sound of song
Be heard in you again.
Nor the voice of bride and bridegroom
Nor the echo of the laborers' din.

Though your merchants were
The world's great men,
By consumption's cult
Through your greed and sin
You'll become a smoking spectacle;
They will weep and mourn and cry

Woe, woe is Babylon,
City of great power;
Behold your doom
You'll be consumed
In one single hour.

CHAPTER ELEVEN

REVELATION 19
THE HOPE OF OUR COMING
WEDDING TO THE LAMB

FROM THE WORD

One of my earliest and most naive prayers as a young Christian was, "Heavenly Father, please do not send Jesus back to the earth before I have a chance to get married." In fact, I had an underlying suspicion that heaven might not quite be as heavenly if you entered it as a single man. Where such a notion came from I cannot tell you!

Well, God answered that prayer. In fact He over-answered it! He brought an amazing woman into my life named Darlene. For a quarter of a century she has been a primary means of God's grace in my life. There have been moments with her in which I have actually pondered, "How could heaven possibly be any better than this?" It did not take a long journey within the boundaries of the state of "marital bliss," however, for me to realize that marriage is a whole lot more than I bargained for! I was totally unprepared for the depth of soul exposure that this relationship brings with it.

To discover how clueless and powerless I was—and still am to a large measure—to really love another human being (especially a wife!), has been overwhelming. My orientation towards self-preoccupation and self-protection had a root system like crabgrass. What was I thinking when I promised with such confidence to love Darlene, "as Christ loved the church and gave Himself up for her"? Looking back through two-and-a-half decades to the evening of May 5, 1972, I believe a good part of my unglorified heart was saying to itself that night, *Finally, I have someone who is going to "fill me up"! I can crawl back into the womb, plug in my umbilical cord, and enjoy the ride! This is going to be great!*

I am so glad our Father is "rich in mercy." I am also thankful for a merciful wife!

Among the many lessons which God has taught me through marriage to a wonderful woman, none is more important than the call to constantly ponder Jesus' love for His bride, the church, of which (I must constantly remind myself) I am a part. The apostle Paul prayed that believers in Ephesus would "have power, together with all the saints, to grasp how wide and long and high and deep is the love of Christ, and to know this love that surpasses knowledge" (Eph. 3:18–19). Only the love of Jesus can "fill us up." There is no spouse or other human being in the world that can possibly meet the deepest longings of our souls. Only Jesus, our perfect and passionate Bridegroom, can satisfy the craving for ultimate intimacy that rages within us. To place this burden upon marriage, or any relationship, is either to make an idol or destroy a friendship. In most cases, it becomes both. I have found that the more I am preoccupied with the inexhaustible love of Christ, the more I move toward my wife to give, rather than to demand.

Another eternally important lesson that the Father has been teaching me as a married man is the joy and freedom that are realized from meditating on the coming "wedding of the Lamb," which brings us to chapter 19 and to a vision calculated to thrill and encourage all Christians who live between the comings of Christ. Just as the theme of spiritual warfare and impending judgment intensifies as John receives more visions of the final phase of history, so the theme of Jesus' love for His bride intensifies in its glory and grandeur! Unfortunately, many Christians get so dogmatically heated in their attempt to set forth the time and details of the second coming that they tend to lose sight of the purpose and beauty of His coming.

Jesus is coming for His bride—His wife to whom He is betrothed, His beloved whom He will forever "have and hold." Let this vision go deep into your heart, for there is no aspect of the gospel that has greater power to bring forth hope and persevering love in the midst of the worst assaults. We are not just going to heaven, we're heading for our wedding celebration and marriage to the Lamb of God, Jesus.

Delighting in the Demise of the Mother of Adulteries—Rev. 19:1–5

How fitting it is that Revelation 19 opens with an awesome worship celebration in response to the destruction of "the great prostitute who corrupted the earth by her adulteries" (19:2). Before the "wedding of the Lamb" we find great rejoicing over God's judgment upon this false lover. Throughout the Scriptures we find God describing His people's love for sin and compromise with "gods" of the surrounding cultures as adultery. When we sin, we do so against His love, not just against His law. God has a holy jealousy for our hearts and for our affection, a jealousy that Abraham Kuyper, former prime minister of the Netherlands, referred to as the greatest compliment God could ever give us. The destruction of Babylon says as much about the love God has for His people as it does about His hatred of evil.

"Hallelujah!" roars a great multitude in heaven. "Salvation

and glory and power belong to our God" (19:1). not to the whore, who vied for the affection of the nations of the world. This is the only chapter in the New Testament in which we find the praise word, "Hallelujah." How appropriate that it would be reserved for a chapter so full of marital metaphors to underscore God's intimate love for the bride. As the smoke rises from Babylon's fiery demise so the praise rises from the "twenty-four elders and the four living creatures" who all fall down and worship God. Then all of the servants of God, "both small and great," are invited to join in the shouting celebration of heaven. This worship service is not just for those who have been martyred. It is for all the people of God. It is for us!

The Marriage of the Lamb: The Bride Is Ready— Rev. 19:6–10

Once again the Revelation whets our appetite for the quality of worship we are going to enjoy throughout eternity. John heard "what sounded like a great multitude, like the roar of rushing waters and like loud peals of thunder, shouting: 'Hallelujah! / For our Lord God Almighty reigns. / Let us rejoice and be glad / and give him glory!'" (19:6).

Again and again and again in Revelation we find the sovereignty of God as a major theme of the worship in heaven. But the great joy of this vision quickly shifts to the good news that a wedding is about to take place. "For the wedding of the Lamb has come, and his bride has made herself ready" (19:7). Jesus is getting ready to receive His bride, His beloved for whom He died. Nothing is left for Him to do except to return for His heart's desire (Eph. 5:25, 32; Matt. 25:1 ff; Mark 2:19; John 3:29; 2 Cor. 11:2).

The bride has made herself ready, as well. "Fine linen [the righteous acts of the saints], bright and clean, was given her to wear" (19:8). Don't let this picture confuse you, as though it were meant to imply that we earn our salvation. Philip Hughes helps us here: "The righteous deeds of the saints . . . do not constitute or contribute to their justification before God, which would be self-justification; as the deeds *of the saints* they are performed by those who are already redeemed and justified in Christ. They are evidence of the bride's sanctification and at the same time of her serious concern to prepare herself for the marriage of the Lamb. This preparedness is effected through the sanctifying work of the Holy Spirit transforming her progressively into the likeness of her Bridegroom"[1] (2 Cor. 3:18; 1 John 3:2 ff; 2 Cor. 5:15; Tit. 2:11–14).

The angel cries out with joy, "Blessed are those who are invited to the wedding supper of the Lamb!" Indeed! What a marriage banquet this is going to be! (Matt. 26:29; Luke 22:28–30). To fully appreciate the meaning of this exquisite passage we need to have a basic understanding of the marriage customs of the Jewish culture in which Jesus was raised. *First, there is the betrothal.* During this period of the relationship the bride and the groom are considered legally to be husband and wife, far more binding than what we know as an "engagement" between a man and a woman. Nothing less than a divorce could dissolve the marriage at this point. The apostle Paul uses this image to describe the relationship that we have with the Lord Jesus this side of His second coming. To the Corinthians he wrote with pastoral concern, "I promised you to one husband, to Christ, so that I might pre-sent you as a pure virgin to him." His fear was that the believers in Corinth might be "led astray" from their "sincere and pure devotion to Christ" (2 Cor. 11:2, 3).

Between the betrothal and the wedding feast came the interval. During this period the groom would pay an agreed-upon dowry to the father of the bride, if this had not already been taken care of. The dowry could be money, animals, goods, or some form of service rendered, as Jacob worked for Rachel (Gen. 29:20). As the interval drew to a close, preparation for the procession would begin. The bride would adorn herself in anticipation of the great celebration and the groom would get dressed in his best attire. With his good friends singing and carrying torches, he would make his way to the home of his betrothed.

After receiving his bride the procession would return to his home or to the home of his parents. At this point the party began! A great feast, including the wedding supper, would last from between seven-to-fourteen days. Very few celebrations could compare with the joy and happiness known at a wedding feast in Jewish culture.

Yet think of it, our wedding feast with Jesus, our Bridegroom, is not going to last a mere seven or fourteen days. It is going to last throughout eternity! Rejoicing with the Love of our lives and with the bride redeemed from every people group in every period of history! What could possibly compare with such a glorious reality? At this point I am reminded of Paul's words when he wrote, "No eye has seen, no ear has heard, no mind has conceived what God has prepared for those who love him" (1 Cor. 2:9). Surely he must have been thinking about our marriage to the Lamb.

As John saw what the angel had to reveal about these matters, he "fell at his feet to worship him." The aged apostle is so overwhelmed by the glory of it all that he simply *has* to worship! But his worship is misdirected toward the angel, who responds, "Do not do it! I am a fellow servant with you and with your brothers who hold to the testimony of Jesus" (19:10). Oh, that such awe would overtake us, as well, as the hope of our wonderful future captures our hearts. We are the bride of Jesus, His betrothed. He cannot love us more! He will not love us less! We are in the wonderful interval period.

There is no dowry left to be paid. The procession is not far away.

This Bridegroom Is a Mighty Warrior—
Rev. 19:11–21

Before Jesus takes His bride into eternity He thoroughly destroys *all* of her adversaries. As the overthrow of Babylon was highlighted in Revelation 18 for the church's encouragement, so now the overthrow of the beast and the false prophet are brought into focus. Every bride thrives in the security of the involved love of a husband who will pay any price to protect and care for her. As the Lamb has paid the supreme price by laying down His own life to purchase His bride, so now He ever lives to care for her. He spares no expense.

Once again heaven is opened to John. Before him is "a white horse, whose rider is called Faithful and True" (19:11). As Jesus came into the world the first time as the suffering Savior, despised and rejected, so the second time He returns as a warrior-judge with "eyes [of] blazing fire." As the "Word of God," He executes the will of God and leads the armies of heaven in conquest. Any concept of spiritual warfare that does not begin with a vision of Jesus as the divine warrior is simply insufficient. He is the One who leads us against His own enemies. We are not fighting for Him, but *with* Him!

From His mouth now comes the pronouncement of final judgment, not the gospel of saving grace. Remember, this Lamb is also a Lion! He is covered with the blood that comes from the execution of justice, recalling Isaiah's prophecy of one who comes "speaking in righteousness, / mighty to save . . . I trampled them in my anger / and trod them down in my wrath; / their blood spattered my garments, / and I stained all my clothing. / For the day of vengence was in my heart, / and the year of my redemption has come" (Isa. 63:1, 3–4). Our Bridegroom is none other than "THE KING OF KINGS AND LORD OF LORDS"! (19:16).

In stark contrast with the "wedding supper of the Lamb," John is now given a vision of the "banquet of the beasts." Birds of prey are summoned together for the "great supper of God," that becomes a hideous feeding frenzy upon the carcasses of the enemies of God overthrown by the Lamb and His armies. The flesh of the "small and the great," the whole world of unbelief, becomes the meal upon which "all the birds gorged themselves." What a sobering picture this is of the judgment that is awaiting those who have "received the mark of the beast and worshiped his image."

HALLELUJAH!

Revelation 19

FROM THE SONG

We have become so "civilized" in our time that it is hard for some of us to imagine rejoicing over the manner in which God exacts His vengeance in Revelation. *How primitive*, we piously think to ourselves. After all, aren't we all sinners? Wouldn't rejoicing over God's punishment be hypocritical?

The truth is that in Scripture, rejoicing is always tied to either what God has done or what He has promised He will do, an event that often includes the destruction of the wicked. He has revealed in His Word that vengeance is His, and His alone, and it is His decision to exact vengeance on the "evil one who corrupted the earth." And it is precisely this that caused the multitude in heaven to begin rejoicing and shouting, "Hallelujah!" No one in the heavenly crowd seemed squeamish about fully celebrating what God has done.

Hallelujah, which literally means "Praise be to Yahweh," is a word one might assume appears numerous times in the Bible. However, we find it primarily in the book of Psalms (104:35; 105:45; 111:1; 112:1; or the great "hallelujah" section from Psalm 146–150) as "Praise the LORD." In the New Testament it is found only in Revelation and is the keynote of the great multitude in heaven in chapter 19.

They shout, "Hallelujah!" not merely over the downfall of the evil one but because of who God is, because of His salvation, power, and glory. They shout, "Hallelujah!" because at last His reign is established forever and the wedding of the Lamb has come!

We shout, "Praise be to Yahweh!" (the literal meaning of "hallelujah") in the midst of the great multitude because if there is a prefect phrase to shout to the Lord, this is it. We rejoice because He approaches on the great white war horse, the sight of which, in itself, is enough to destroy the wicked.

Hallelujah!

Hallelujah! Hallelujah!
Salvation and power and glory
Belong to our God
Amen!
Hallelujah! Hallelujah!
The evil one who corrupted the earth
Is condemned.

Death for the dark adulteress
Destroyed at last forever,

And by His judgments, just and true,
He has avenged the blood
Of all His saints.

Hallelujah! Hallelujah!
The Lord God Almighty has come
Now forever to reign.
Amen!
Hallelujah! Hallelujah!
Let all those who love Him
Give glory, rejoice, and be glad.

The wedding of the Lamb has come;
His bride has made herself ready.
And she shall wear linen bright and clean
Woven of the faithful acts
Of the saints.

King of Kings
and Lord of Lords,
King of Kings
And Lord of Lords.
(repeat)

CHAPTER TWELVE

REVELATION 20
THE HOPE OF THE ALREADY
AND NOT YET

FROM THE WORD

All of my life I have heard the phrase, "It's all Greek to me," to express bewilderment or utter consternation. The clear impression is that "Greek" is a very difficult language since it has become a metaphor for the impossible. Therefore, it was with much fear and trepidation that I enrolled in my first course of this ancient and "dead" language during the final semester of my senior year at North Carolina. I had struggled to get through Spanish! How was I going to learn the dialect of Aristotle and Plato? My anxieties were only heightened by the fact that this was going to be a course in Koine Greek, the "street" form of the language used by the authors of the New Testament. Therefore, I concluded, if I failed this course any hopes of ever really understanding the Scriptures would be forever forfeited, and I would be labeled a biblical illiterate, disqualified for ministry. Oh, the power of an unbridled imagination fed by clichés from the past!

Well, much to my surprise and joy, I made an A in the class. I wasn't learning how to order supper at a cafe in Athens, I was learning to read and study God's Word. But I also give much credit to an outstanding professor whose love for the Scriptures, the Lord, and his students was quite pronounced.

I not only learned more Greek than I anticipated from a three-hour introductory course, I also learned a little Latin to boot! Alongside a new syntax, grammar, and vocabulary, we were given some basic skills in New Testament hermeneutics and exegesis. This included being introduced to a different phenomenon in the text of the New Testament: the *hapax legomena*, a word or group of words that occurs only one time in the New Testament. Occasionally an author of a book in the New Testament may have used a particular Greek word or phrase that can be found nowhere else in the other books. The importance of such details for interpreting the Scriptures should be obvious. Why would an author only use this particular word or phrase just once? Why wasn't it used by other writers? What special care should we take in interpreting this part of God's Word?

These questions are relevant as we come to a concept specifically mentioned in only one chapter, not just in the New Testament, but in the whole Bible. In Revelation 20 we are told of a "thousand year" reign of Jesus, known best by its Latin name, the "millennium." Historically, there have been very few, if any, issues born out of a study of the book of Revelation that have caused more strife and division between Christians.

Now some of you more trained than I in textual criticism and knowledge of Greek will argue that the "one thousand years" in Revelation 20 is technically not a *hapax legomena* at all, for John uses the phrase six times in the chapter and the apostle Peter tells us that "With the Lord a day is like a thousand years, and a thousand years are like a day" (2 Pet. 3:8). Picky, picky, picky!

My concern is not to argue that point at all. What I am

most zealous for us to ponder is the importance of being very careful about being overly dogmatic about such a huge concept about which we are given so little information in God's Word. Wisdom would seem to encourage us towards the "lean rather than luxurious" school of interpretation over a concept like the millennium. Let us look at this wonderful thousand-year period in the context of the whole book of Revelation and seek to understand how John's original audience would have been deeply encouraged from this grand vision.

THE THOUSAND YEARS— REV. 20:1–15

As John has already been given graphic insight into the destruction of the dragon's allies and emissaries of evil, so next he is shown the present and future state of the lord of evil, Satan himself. An angel comes down from heaven, "having the key to the Abyss and holding in his hand a great chain." Authority over the place of the dead, the "Abyss," is centered in heaven, not in hell. Let us never forget this. This mighty angel takes his chain and seizes the dragon, that ancient serpent, who is the devil, or Satan, and binds him for a thousand years. Once again we are reminded that Satan is not autonomous. It doesn't take a thousand angels to do this binding; only one! But immediately the questions in our hearts as we read this text are, "What is meant by this thousand-year period?" "How does the millennium relate to the second coming of Jesus?" These questions, and others generated by Revelation 20, bring us to the place of presenting a basic overview and the highlights of the three main schools of millennial thought that have been developed by thinking Christians in church history. It is important to note that each of these three schools of interpretation is represented by men and women who affirm the absolute inspiration and authority of the Bible—our brothers and sisters who have lived and died for the glory of Jesus Christ.

Premillennialism

This position is born out of a belief that the book of Revelation is to be interpreted as "literally" as possible. Numbers and images are to be taken at face value unless a symbolic intent is clearly obvious. Premillennialists also stress the importance of accepting the sequence in which John received his visions as the sequence in which these events will happen in history. Thus, this school of interpretation maintains that the "one thousand years" of John's vision is to be taken as an actual, measurable period. Central to premillennialism is the conviction that Jesus Christ will return to earth in order to inaugurate this long season of peace and righteousness; thus, the name pre-millennialism.

The millennium is a period in which Jesus will literally reign upon the earth with His people. At the beginning of this era of triumph, Satan is bound, the first resurrection of Christians occurs, and the kingdom rule of the Lamb is manifest throughout the earth. After a thousand years Satan will be set free, and he will make a final attempt to deceive the nations and attack the saints. This rebellion leads to the final showdown between his kingdom and the Kingdom of God, during which Satan and his allies will be utterly defeated and thrown into the lake of fire. The second resurrection will take place along with the final judgment. This will mark the beginning of the final state: the ushering in of the new heavens and the new earth for God's children and eternal perdition for those who have refused His grace. These are the basic elements of premillennialism although there is a variety of different schools within this one system.

Postmillennialism

This view maintains that John's vision of a thousand-year period refers to an exponentially growing state of peace, prosperity, and victory, which the gospel will effect throughout the world *before* Jesus returns to the earth. Those who hold to this school emphasize the prophecies of the Old Testament that speak of the advancement of the gospel throughout the world, not just with respect to the conversion of many from every nation, but also to the "healing of the nations." Postmillennialists believe that we should work, pray, hope, and expect a near Christianizing of the world prior to the return of Christ. Many who have historically held to this position on the millennium lived through great revivals and reformations in their lifetime, leading them to believe that God will accomplish the same, universally, as a testimony to the power of the gospel and the glory of Jesus Christ.

Amillennialism

Amillennialism maintains that the thousand years are to be taken metaphorically, consistent with the use of numbers found throughout the book of Revelation. Therefore, there is no calendar-calculated millennium, per se; thus, the name "amillennium." Rather, this period is understood to represent the entire period of time between the comings of Christ, which we have been referring to as the "interadvent" period. It is seen as describing the present reign of Christ from heaven with His saints, both in heaven and on the earth. Jesus is acknowledged to be the King of Kings and Lord of

Lords *now*, having ascended to the right hand of the Father after His resurrection.

Amillennialists emphasize the great defeat of Satan by Jesus upon His cross. The "binding" of the arch enemy, therefore, refers to his no longer being able to keep the nations of the world deceived about the great salvation of our God. Thus, during this period of history heaven is being filled up with men and women, not just from among the Jewish nation, but also from every nation and people upon the face of the earth.

The "first resurrection," in this school of interpretation, refers to the resurrection of Jesus Christ, in which all Christians share by virtue of their union with Him. At the end of history Satan will be "loosed," that is, again he will be given power briefly to deceive and blind the nations, setting the stage for a final conflict and spiritual war that will precipitate his absolute defeat by the return of Jesus Christ. Then comes the "second resurrection," at which time all men will be raised from the dead to face the final judgment. For those whose names are not "written in the book of life," there will be the "second death," the eternal state of misery defined by the absolute absence of the presence of God.

What's *Your* Position?

How, then, are we to choose from among these options? Once again let me acknowledge that each of these positions has been held and is currently championed by Christians who hold the Scriptures to be the inspired Word of God, inerrant, and fully authoritative as the only rule of faith and life that God has given His people. Our decision is not a matter of choosing between conservative and liberal theological schools of biblical interpretation. This cannot be emphasized too much.

In my own journey in the land of millennial options and confusion, here are some conclusions I have reached:

Because my heroes, mentors, and teachers—in print and in life—have come from each of these schools of interpretation I have felt no pressure to reach a dogmatic ironclad conclusion on "my position." The very fact that men and women whom I love and respect so much in the Lord have settled into different millennial camps has actually brought freedom rather than confusion to my heart as I ponder the meaning of Revelation 20.

Our participation and enjoyment of the millennium is not tied to our particular interpretation and position. No Christian is going to be left out or disappointed! No amillennialist is going to pout if the postmillennialist is right. No postmillennialist is going to have his feelings hurt if amillennialism proves to be more consistent with the unfolding of the history of redemption. Premillennialists are not going to high five one another for a thousand years in the face of dejected postmils and amils, should their view on these matters be realized in history. The good news is that all Christians are all going to enjoy fully everything won for us by our blessed Lord and Savior, Jesus Christ, no matter what our position on the millennium is! I have stressed this truth with our church family, not to diminish the zeal for millennial study and discussion but rather to see that same zeal expended on the advancement of the gospel of the kingdom of God among the nations of the world and in our own culture.

There is much to be learned and appreciated about each of the three main millennial positions. They all affirm that the best is yet to come, that the millennium is leading to the glories of the return of Jesus Christ for His beloved bride, the church. Christians in each of these millennial camps long for the fulfillment of all of God's promises and prophecies to be realized fully only in heaven itself.

Benefiting from Each of the Millennial Positions

Let us, then, respect how committed the premillennialist is to the "plain sense of the text." The words of the Bible are to be treated as they really are, the very words of God Himself. This position is held by those who share a common concern not to let the text of Revelation be overly spiritualized or simply treated as a recording of John's mystical experiences from which we draw allegories and principles. We should also appreciate the future orientation of this view. History is heading toward the consummation of all things with the time-and-space return of Jesus Christ to the earth, a return which may be in our lifetime! All of life is to be lived in light of the hope of His coming. This emphasis is sometimes lost in the other millennial positions.

The postmillennialist encourages us to ponder the power the gospel has in all spheres of life: politics, education, economics, the arts, and society. Believing that the good news of Jesus Christ is much more than the means by which we can go to heaven one day, the postmil bids us take very seriously our calling to be salt and light in a world over which our God reigns with absolute sovereignty. The optimism of the postmil is a helpful corrective to those Christians who have allowed their hearts to be filled with more fear than faith as they ponder the future. Our postmil brethren invite us to study the Reformation and some of the great revivals, like the Great Awakening, which God has brought to His people, that our hearts might be stirred with confident faith and courageous expectancy as we approach the nations of the world as ambassadors of Christ.

The amillennialist helps us avoid the extremes of faithless pessimism and exaggerated optimism by acknowledging that the Scriptures teach that the wheat and the tares are going to grow together until Jesus returns. The clash

between the kingdom of God and the kingdom of darkness
will continue until the King Himself returns. The amil also
invites us to consider the significance of the ascension and
current reign of the Lord Jesus over all things. We are not
waiting for Him to become the Lord of Lords and the King
of Kings. He already is. Amillennialism is driven by a vision
of the work of Jesus upon the cross by which Satan has been
defeated and through which men and women from every
people group in history are being redeemed. We can benefit
tremendously from the amil's biblical worldview which hon-
ors God as Creator and Redeemer and calls the church to be
involved in the culture with a redemptive presence.

The Already and the Not Yet

As I was working through this section of Revelation with
our church family and discussing the various evangelical millennial options, I literally saw peace and joy move across the
room like a gentle and calming breeze. For many, this was
the first time to hear that faithful Christians have held dif-
fering positions on the millennium throughout the history of
the Church. Once again, we enjoyed watching many of our
theological stereotypes and caricatures crumble under the
weight of openness and the study of both the Scripture and
the history of interpretation of these things. Even those
Christians in our fellowship who have come from the most
hardened and dogmatic millennial backgrounds conceded
that mutual respect and humility are called for as we discuss
this important part of biblical revelation with one another.
What matters most today is not what position we take in the
ongoing millennial debates. What matters is for each of us to
ponder how our position is affecting the way we live life to
the glory of God. If any one of these understandings of the

millennium is taken seriously, then all of life will be noticeably altered and redirected for the purposes of eternity.

As I was bringing this discussion to a conclusion, I should have anticipated what was about to happen. In the back of the Art House I saw a hand shoot up just as I was heading toward the closing prayer. "Pastor Scotty, this section on the millennium has been really helpful to me, but I still don't know where *you* stand. Would you mind briefly giving us *your* position, or at least which one of these you are most drawn to?"

My first reaction was to offer to talk privately with this individual after the study. But that seemed to be the easy way out, the course of least resistance! Then I realized what a great opportunity this was to encourage the group to wrestle with the biblical information for themselves. As a pastor I take great delight when those who sit under my teaching and preaching prove to be like the Bereans in Paul's day who examined the Scriptures night and day to confirm whether or not what he was teaching was really according to God's Word. That is all that really matters.

I describe myself as a "functional amil." After reading the Revelation over and over I have been led to embrace the essence of the amillennial position with certain qualifications. Throughout Revelation two main themes have captured my attention and heart:

First is the occupied throne of heaven. Our God reigns! The triumph of Jesus upon the cross and His resurrection from the grave are more clear and glorious to me than ever. Jesus is exalted to the right hand of the Father. He is already King of Kings and Lord of Lords! Nothing can hinder or alter our God's redemptive purposes. As I have highlighted throughout this book, God is filling up heaven with men and women from every race, tribe, and tongue. My soul rejoices and rests in the advancement of the gospel. Satan's stronghold has been broken!

Second, every verse of every chapter invokes the longing in my heart for the return of Him for whose glory I have been made and by whose grace I have been set eternally free. Although I can hardly wait to see Jesus and to be made like Him in every respect, I know I must; but I am overwhelmed as I fill my heart with visions of the new heavens and the new earth.

This is why I call myself a "functional amillennialist." I appreciate very much the emphasis that amillennialism places on the current exaltation and reign of Jesus Christ over all things. I am also drawn to the understanding that the binding of Satan primarily refers to the fruitful preaching of the gospel among the nations of the world.

But I also love the punctilious emphasis of the premillennialist on the imminent return of Jesus to the world. Many amillennialists simply do not seem to emphasize this anticipation, expectancy, and love for the appearing of our Lord as much as the Scriptures encourage. This is why I refer to myself as a *functional amil.*

My understanding of the millennium really makes a difference in the way I respond to the gospel. It is no mere theological label and handshake that I use to distinguish myself from other millennial fraternities.

So this tension of the "already and the not yet" thrills my heart and feeds my passion. "Already" the kingdom of Jesus has broken into the world. He has accomplished a mighty victory over sin, death, and Satan upon His cross. He has poured forth His Spirit, and we are participating in the great harvest of men and women as the gospel goes forth throughout the world. But, "not yet" do we enjoy the fullness of the kingdom and of life as it will only be known when King Jesus returns. Therefore, my millennial view functions to propel me to rest in His reign and, at the same time, long for His return.

My "position" is perhaps best expressed in the words of the apostle Paul when he wrote to Christians in Rome: "We know that the whole creation has been groaning as in the pains of childbirth right up to the present time. Not only so, but we ourselves, who have the firstfruits of the Spirit, groan inwardly as we wait eagerly for our adoption as sons, the redemption of our bodies. For in this hope we were saved" (Rom. 8:22–24).

The redemptive tension of "groaning inwardly and waiting eagerly" best summarizes my heart as I reflect on all biblical revelation. Jesus reigns; Jesus shall reign! That's all I need to know. I am being more completely captured by the enormity of His cross and the depth of His love. And I am also being made increasingly aware of the fact that in this world I have no lasting city. I want the firstfruits of the Spirit to give way to the fullness of the feast! I so wish Jesus would return by this afternoon, even before I put a period at the end of this sentence. But if His sovereign and saving purposes are best served by the delay of His return for another thousand years, I will also rejoice and be glad. Hallelujah, what a Savior! Hallelujah, what a salvation!

CHAPTER THIRTEEN

REVELATION 21–22
THE HOPE OF THE NEW HEAVENS
AND THE NEW EARTH

FROM THE WORD

What a day! A steady breeze is blowing, which is causing the forest of blue-green spruce trees on the hills in front of me to hum a most relaxing melody. I'm just this side of chilly. The leaves of the Aspen trees are dancing in time with every variation of the tempo of the early morning wind. Huge mountains, capped with the residue of winter snow, are straining, reaching up toward one of the most beautiful skies I have ever seen.

A brilliantly intense sun is ducking in and out from behind the clouds, painting the mountains with an ever-changing array of shadows and hues. Ground squirrels are running from burrow to burrow only stopping long enough to forage for a little breakfast. It's good to be here.

No, I didn't fly to Switzerland to write the last chapter of this book. Rather, I'm in the Colorado Rockies, to be specific, in Estes Park, just a little way from Rocky Mountain National Park, one of the most incredible pieces of real estate lovingly preserved and meticulously cared for by our federal government's parks system. How fitting it is that I would be here, with the Rockies in full view, to write about our forever home. For John is taken up to a high mountain that he might view the wonders of what eye has not seen, ear has not heard, the mind of man has not even imagined. God purposes to engage every faculty that He has given us as He makes His heart and our heavenly hope known to us. Indeed, as we have witnessed throughout John's pastoral prophecy, it is a revelation in sight and sound—not just in word. This is nowhere more obvious than in the way God describes heaven for us. He wants us to see, hear, understand, and feel our awesome destiny. Our inheritance. Our future. Our glory. Home.

That our Lord completes His written Word (not just the book of Revelation) with this magnificent vision of heaven is worth pondering. Last words are lasting words. Final images are powerful images. God wants our hearts to be consumed with a vision of our forever. It is simply not true that we can be so "heavenly minded, we are of no earthly good." I decry that trite maxim as much as I hate the bumper sticker that says, "God is my co-pilot." The more I study the Scriptures and church history the more I am convinced that those who are captured by this vision of heaven are significantly and sacrificially committed to living redemptively in the world. It is also they who live like God is God, and not merely a co-pilot.

The apostle Paul was thrilled and empowered by just such a vision. It was a vision of heaven that transformed Paul's whole experience of pain and suffering. To the Philippians he penned these words from prison, "For to me, to live is Christ and to die is gain. If I am to go on living in the body, this will mean fruitful labor for me. Yet what shall I choose? I do not know! I am torn between the two: I desire to depart and be with Christ, which is better by far" (Phil. 1:21–23). Though he preferred heaven, heaven preferred that Paul stay and minister to the saints in Philippi. With joy, he agreed.

The Puritan clergyman Richard Baxter recommended in his classic, *The Saints' Everlasting Rest*, that Christians meditate on heaven thirty minutes every day! What began as his own funeral sermon, written as he felt very near to his own death, went on to become a volume that has brought great encouragement for the last 350 years.

But it's not merely the thought of heaven that matters. It is heaven itself that matters. As important as it is to think about our eternal dwelling with God, what we think of this glorious state of existence is even more important. As a pastor for the last twenty years, I believe that most American Christians are noticeably uninformed about the biblical account of heaven. Oh, how our hearts and lives are the poorer for it.

Where do we typically learn about the afterlife? Much of my own early imaging of the eternal state came from Saturday morning cartoons, bad hymns, TV, movies, and paper-goods commercials. I remember thinking that everybody who goes there must become an angel, because that's who was always depicted as inhabiting the afterlife. Cherublike little children, floating on white clouds, were mingled in with older, wiser, slow-moving, slow-talking angels. The atmosphere of heaven always seemed misty and surreal. The music was an annoying blend of soprano choirs accompanied by poor harpists. God, if represented at all, spoke with a deep, synthesized voice, more robotic than inviting. His being was never personalized, only presented as a bright light on a distant throne. Why I ever wanted to go to such a place, I do not know. Maybe because it just seemed better than the alternative!

At age eleven, however, thinking about life after death took on a new importance. I came home from school one day in the fall of my sixth-grade year to the tragic news that my mother had been killed in an automobile accident. All of a sudden angels, harps, and clouds meant nothing to me. Not being a Christian at the time, I had no spiritual resources to draw upon. Older well-meaning friends tried to comfort me with statements like, "Your mom is in a better place." Such words served more as a panacea for my stunned, broken, and confused little heart, than they reflected any meaningful belief in heaven. Silly, sentimental images of my mother "having fun" were used in an attempt to deaden the pain of her being ripped from my everyday life. It wasn't until seven years later, when I became a Christian, that I began to understand the substantive reality and living hope of that which our Father has in store for us. Although I wasn't a Christian when my mom died, she was.

In the last two chapters of Revelation, we are not given an exhaustive picture of our existence in eternity, but we are given a sufficient one—indeed, a most inviting one. As our imagination is captured by this vision of heaven, we, too, will say with Paul "to depart would be better by far."

The New Heavens and the New Earth

"Then I saw a new heaven and a new earth, for the first heaven and the first earth had passed away, and there was no longer any sea" (21:1). As the first book of the Bible, Genesis, begins with the story of God's first creation, the last book finishes with the hope of God's new creation. All of my childhood and, I must confess, a good part of my adult Christian life, I always assumed that heaven existed somewhere "up there," in some remote, beautiful place beyond the Milky Way. I figured that if you "go to heaven," of course, you have to leave the environs of our terra firma. And most certainly, in a very real and blessed sense, Christians who have died before the return of Jesus Christ "go to be with the Lord." For the Scriptures teach us that "to be absent from the body is to be present with the Lord."

Those who have died "in the Lord" are not in a soul sleep, awaiting the day of resurrection. They are enjoying rich communion with the living and loving Triune God and with all members of the "church triumphant." Yet as wonderful as their experience is now, it is not complete. They have yet to enter in to the full inheritance that will be the eternal portion of the people of God after Jesus Christ returns to the earth to precipitate the final estate of all things eternal. There is a deep longing in our hearts for this day that no other set of circumstances can satisfy.

And it is not just God's people, both living and dead, who await the full harvest. Paul wrote to the Romans, "The creation waits in eager expectation for the sons of God to be revealed. For the creation was subjected to frustration, not by its own choice, but by the will of the one who subjected it, in hope that the creation itself will be liberated from its bondage to decay and brought into the glorious freedom of the children of God" (Rom. 8:19–21).

The scope of the salvation that filled Paul's heart is much broader and more comprehensive than the one that fills our horizons. The atoning death of the Lamb of God, Jesus, is so powerful and magnificent that it not "merely" effects the liberation of God's people from every people group in history, it will also bring about the ushering in of the "new heaven and the new earth"! Such a notion flies in the face of the prevailing worldview surrounding the first-century church. The Greeks exalted "spirit" to the deprecation of "matter." But the Bible bids us celebrate and honor God who is Creator even before He reveals Himself as Redeemer. How instructive it is for us to realize that heaven, as God has decreed, includes not just the world of spirit but also the material world that He has created to reflect His glory.

Putting these Scriptures together, it is more accurate to say that heaven is going to come to us rather than to say that we are going to heaven! According to Scriptures, our eternal celebration is not going to take place somewhere up in the clouds, but, rather, right here in God's world, which will be totally remade and renewed. As I began writing this book I commented that if the new creation is no more beautiful than my beloved Switzerland, I would be a satisfied man. But I have a deep sense and full expectation that when the present creation is "liberated from its bondage," I am going to have to repent of being far too easily satisfied. There is no way that our preglorified senses can begin to take in the full glory of the "new creation." The Swiss Alps are but a dull shadow of what is ahead!

One more thing needs to be mentioned about the incomparable new world that is coming. John's words, "and there was no longer any sea," used to deeply trouble me. I thought, *How will the new heaven and new earth be that awesome without oceans and great beaches?* And then I realized that for John the "sea" is a metaphor for chaos and evil. The "seven-headed beast" of chapter 13 came "out of the sea" and the great prostitute of chapter 17 "sits on many waters." It's not the absence of crashing waves upon white shorelines that will be eradicated, but everything that is indicative of turmoil. It will not surprise me to find the beauty of the beaches of the new earth far surpassing anything we have known before, even in Hawaii!

The Immanuel Principle: Relationship with God Perfected

The next aspect of our eternal blessedness concerns God's perfected relationship with us, His beloved. In fact the majority of what God makes known about heaven in these two final chapters of Revelation is its relational beauty. A loud voice from "the throne" announces, "Now the dwelling of God is with men, and he will live with them. They will be his people, and God himself will be with them and be their God" (21:3). As awesome and completely satisfying as the beauty of the new heavens and the new earth is, that which will make heaven most heavenly will be the way our Father relates to us. Even as He has already perfectly reconciled Himself to us, and us to Him, through the death of Jesus, nevertheless, there awaits the fulfillment of the promises that have stood ever since Adam and Eve rebelled against His love in the garden of Eden. The "Immanuel theme," by which God pledges to be with and for His people, runs throughout the Old Testament (Lev. 26:11–12; Jer. 31:33; Ezek. 37:27; Zech. 8:8). John is given a tantalizing glimpse of the Father's affection for His children.

"'He will wipe every tear from their eyes. There will be no more death or mourning or crying or pain, for the old order of things has passed away.' He who was seated on the throne said, 'I am making everything new!'" (21:4–5). The Greek literally means that God will "wipe out of" our eyes every tear. He who renews all things, redeems all things.

As I mentioned in an earlier chapter, perhaps the first thousand years in this timeless state will find each of us learning the reasons behind the pain, mourning, and crying we experienced in this life. I can hear the sound of understanding, joy, and relief swelling up from the multinational people of God, "Oh, so that is what You were doing, Father! That which I despised and could never harmonize with a belief in Your mercy and might, I now know to have been a means by which You brought glory to Yourself. Now I see and I praise the mystery of Your providence and ways! Thank You, my God, thank You!" At that time we will enjoy the full the meaning of Paul's words: "Now I know in part; then I shall know fully, even as I am fully known" (1 Cor. 13:12).

Lest these images be interpreted as the hyperbolic wishes of a depressed apostle in exile on Patmos, God puts His own pledge and stamp of authority on such promises of paradise. He instructs John to "Write this down, for these words are trustworthy and true. It is done. I am the Alpha and the Omega, the Beginning and the End" (21:5–6). There is nothing more to be done to secure this blessed state for God's people. Therefore the great invitation once again goes out, "To him who is thirsty I will give to drink without cost from the spring of the water of life" (21:6). The price has been paid. All we have to do is to drink!

Here Comes the Bride: The New Jerusalem

I relish the way the Bible mixes metaphors. It gives me a certain satisfaction if not revenge on all of my high school English teachers who used to give me lower grades for resorting to "confusing imagery." John has already identified the "Holy City, the new Jerusalem, coming down out of heaven" as the "bride beautifully dressed for her husband" (21:2). This picture is now highlighted and developed as one of the seven angels "who had the seven bowls full of the seven last plagues" carries the apostle "in the Spirit to a mountain great and high." This is probably the same angel who had taken John into the wilderness to behold the destruction of the great whore, Babylon (Rev. 17). Now the seer from Patmos is given a mountain-high vantage point so as to behold the brilliance and beauty of the wife of the Lamb.

Another of my cherished, but wrong, notions of heaven is challenged by this section of Scripture. All my life I thought that we Christians would be spending eternity walking on streets of gold, having gone through the pearly white gates into the eternal city whose cubical walls are made of all kinds of precious jewels. And if we were really fortunate our "mansion" would be "next door to Jesus." Now I find out that *we,* the wife of Jesus, are the city! How are we to understand the meaning of such a vision? Once again we need to realize that John's numbers and images are best understood as well-chosen symbols to be meditated upon, rather than as literal visions to be mechanically reproduced.

It seems that through this picture of the "wife who is the new Jerusalem" God is most zealous for us to celebrate at least two great truths: First, we are given a picture of the perfected bride of Christ, the glorified church. How stunning and encouraging such an image must have been for the seven fledgling churches spread around Asia Minor. She who is so small and despised will one day glow, not with the beauty of Cinderella, but with the very glory of God! Our Father wants us to live with the assured hope of our coming glorification. He who began a good work in us will bring it to completion on the day of Jesus' return. Such knowledge and assurance empowers us to thrive and not just survive until our Lord returns for His bride.

This description of the new Jerusalem (21:10–21) is replete with precise measurements, numbers, jewels, precious metals, splendor, and details that are rich in symbolic meaning. The bride-city is fifteen hundred miles in length, breadth, and in height. But how can a city be a cube? Bruce Metzger comments, "The description is architecturally preposterous, and must not be taken with flat-footed literalism. In ancient time the cube was held to be the most perfect of all geometric forms. By this symbolism, therefore, John wants us to understand that the heavenly Jerusalem is absolutely splendid, with a harmony and symmetry of perfect proportions."[1]

Second, our Lord once again emphasizes fulfilled relationship with His people in this magnificent description of the

Jerusalem, seen from on high. John notes, "I did not see a temple in the city, because the Lord God Almighty and the Lamb are its temple" (21:22). According to 1 Kings, which contains a detailed description of the temple Solomon built in Jerusalem, the Holy of Holies measured twenty cubits by twenty cubits by twenty cubits. The Holy of Holies was the place where the presence of God was most profoundly manifest among His covenant people. Surely John's readers would have caught the significance of this image. The life of heaven can best be understood as an intensely intimate and joyous relationship with God. The whole city becomes the Holy of Holies. The bride is perfected in righteousness and God's shekinah radiates the whole realm through the Lamb! The gates are never closed because fellowship and communion with God will never cease. Everyone whose name is written in the Lamb's book of life is welcome.

The City with the Heart of a Garden

The angel next showed John "the river of the water of life, as clear as crystal, flowing from the throne of God and of the Lamb down the middle of the great street of the city." A massive tree, "the tree of life, bearing twelve crops of fruit, yielding its fruit every month," straddles the river on both sides. The foliage of the tree is "for the healing of the nations" (22:1–2). It takes no biblical giant to recognize the intended correlation between this garden and the Garden of Eden. That which was forfeited by sin in the first garden is now restored beyond measure in the garden of the New Jerusalem. Israel's prophets longed for the day when living waters would flow from Jerusalem in the Messianic age (Ezek. 47:1–12; Zech. 14:8). Philip Hughes comments, "The river with its water of life symbolizes the inexhaustible grace of God."[2] As we have already seen, this is the very stream of refreshment to which the Lamb leads His loved ones throughout eternity (7:17).

The "tree of life," whose fruit Adam and Eve were forbidden to eat after the Fall, now becomes the "year-round" symbol of the nourishing heart of "the throne of God and of the Lamb," which are centered in the garden-city. The leaves of the great tree remind us that in heaven the "healing of the nations" will come to completion. The substantive healing that we can know in this life through God's grace will give way to the fullness of His shalom in eternity.

"No longer will there be any curse" (22:3). In this one promise we realize that John is envisioning paradise regained. The curse that our federal parents, Adam and Eve, brought upon themselves and the whole creation is now lifted. Never will we forget that such a blessing is due entirely to the work of the Lamb.

"They will see his face . . ." (22:4). John's readers may have cupped their hands over their mouths with longing wonderment at the thought of such a possibility. For Moses to have seen the face of God would have meant death; for us in heaven, it will mean a level of intimacy, joy, and fellowship with our Lord that we can only imagine from afar.

". . . And his name will be on their foreheads" (22:4). There will be none unknown or unloved in our eternal state of blessedness. For just as "the ground is level at the foot of the cross," so in heaven there will be no pecking order or hierarchy. In the economy of eternity every one of us is precious in the sight of our Father. It will take heaven to finally convince us of this!

How shall we be occupied in this perfected state of relationship with God and one another? Floating on clouds, strumming harps? How boring! According to the Scriptures, we will "serve him" and "reign for ever and ever." The entirety of eternity can simply be called "worship service." In heaven we will finally be free to obey the greatest of all commandments: to love the Lord our God with everything that we have and are. Free at last, free at last, thank God Almighty, we will be free at last.

THE NEW JERUSALEM

Revelation 21

FROM THE SONG

As the great undoing comes full circle, John sees a "new heaven and a new earth." We understand that what seemed the terrible, ultimate end is actually the luminous beginning—that the *bereshith* of Genesis was really only a word from the wings. That first phrase of the Old Testament now echoes back, full of new meaning, in the final fulfillment of the New.

The center of this new creation is the New Jerusalem, the new capital for the ancient King, the bride for the Bridegroom. If Babylon was the wicked whore, Jerusalem is the spotless bride. If Babylon was stumbling toward sudden, eternal destruction, Jerusalem is proceeding to the final, everlasting wedding. The place called the "City of Peace," which has for the last several thousand years been anything but peaceful, will at last live up to her name.

Here the great hope at the center of the heart of God becomes a reality. Here at last He will walk with us and be our God; and we shall be His people. Here He will finally reach out His hand, touch our faces, wipe our tears. For as the loud voice proclaims, "At last the dwelling of God is with men and women, and He will live with them." It has not always been our hope, but it has always been His—from the moment He breathed life into Adam and watched with excitement as he came to life in the garden.

"I am making everything new!" He proclaims. And it is impossible not to hear the thrill in the thunder that is His voice. And behold everything is new! The heavens are ablaze, the earth a verdant paradise. And we have become brilliant beings that we might have been tempted to worship in our old, earthly existence. The river of life is there to quench our thirst, the eternal Sabbath to ease our weariness. The light of God Himself illumines our new world. Above all, His presence—palpable, electric, sizzling—is in the air around us.

We, as children, have experienced the reality of our earthly father's presence in our rooms as we drifted off to sleep. There was the familiar smell of his aftershave, the sounds of his breathing and moving about the room. The knowledge that he was there was all the comfort we needed to drift off to sleep.

Now, as we wake forever, there is another Presence, not so unlike the other. It is our heavenly Father. We can smell the aroma of His glory. We can hear the comforting sounds of His rumblings. And even when He is not before our eyes, the knowledge that He is at last fully there is all the comfort we can bear. "Never will I leave you, never will I forsake you," we hear the thunder whispering as we settle into eternity.

The New Jerusalem

I saw the Holy City
Descending from the sky
So brilliant with the light of God
The City is His bride.

There is no temple in this town
No sun, no moon, no lamp
for God's own glory is its light
Illuminated by the Lamb.

And God Himself will wipe the tears
From every weeping eye,
No death, no pain, no mourning cry
And every tear made dry.
And now our God will dwell with them,
The new Jerusalem.
And He Himself will walk with them
The new Jerusalem.

And so let all of those who thirst
Come now and drink for free
And to the One who overcomes,
Come now and you will see.
Behold the old has passed away,
Now everything is new;
The Alpha and Omega's words
Are trustworthy and so true.

REVELATION 22:6–21
THE HOPE OF
THE GOSPEL

FROM THE WORD

The question that initially stirred within me as I anticipated writing the final chapter of *Unveiled Hope* was, "How can I faithfully and creatively represent the awesome ending of the book of Revelation in an epilogue?" Then it occurred to me that Revelation 22:6–21 is more than John's closing words as he completes the Revelation, it is how God, the primary author and architect of the Bible, chose to conclude the entire Bible!

Sixty-six books, written by forty different human authors over a period of fifteen hundred years . . . and here are the closing thoughts, the final expressions from the heart of God. Last words are lasting words. What does our Father want to impress upon our hearts?

As John is overwhelmed by the sights and sounds of "the new Jerusalem," an angel boldly affirms, "These words are trustworthy and true. The Lord, the God of the spirits of the prophets, sent his angel to show his servants the things that *must* soon take place" (22:6, emphasis mine). This stamp of Divine authority and trustworthiness is critical. John has not merely received some esoteric mystical experience. What he has seen, what he has heard, and what he has written finds its source in God. We can stake our lives on it.

Next, the actual voice of Jesus breaks in, "Behold, I am coming soon! Blessed is he who keeps the words of the prophecy in this book" (22:7). This declaration by Jesus, coupled with the lingering effects of the vision of heaven, are too much for John to absorb. The only appropriate response to the splendor of eternity and this thrilling announcement of our Lord is—worship. Spontaneously, John falls down in adoring prostration at the feet of the angelic messenger, who responds, "Do not do it! I am a fellow servant with you and with your brothers the prophets and of all who keep the words of this book. Worship God!" (22:9)

This is the second time John has received this loving rebuke. He had been so moved by the worship of heaven in response to the fall of Babylon and the announcement of the wedding supper of the Lamb, that he had fallen down in worship of same angel (Rev. 19:9–10). But as Revelation states, worship is never to be given to any creature, angelic or human, only to God Himself. He, alone, is worthy.

The angel continues to instruct John, exhorting him "not [to] seal up the words of the prophecy of this book, because the time is near" (22:10). The implications of the angel's words are clear and important: The book of Revelation is neither exclusively about the distant future nor is it written merely for an elitist few. It is for all of God's "servants," for all "who keep the words of this book."

"The time is near." According to the Scriptures, the "last days" include the entire period between the two comings of Christ. His return is always imminent, but the specific day is known only in the heart of God. How wise of our God to structure the final phase in the history of redemption in a way that keeps us from being either presumptuous or lethargic! We cannot know the day, but we must not ignore the day of Jesus' return.

"Behold, I am coming soon!" (22:12). Jesus addresses these words to Christians and non-Christians alike, to those who "do wrong" and to those who "do right," to the "vile" and to the "holy" (22:11). With Jesus will come the strict justice of the final judgment. All of history, as we know it, is leading unalterably to this Day. Jesus will reward every man "according to what he has done" (22:12). In placing His signature—"the Alpha and the Omega, the First and the Last, the Beginning and the End" (22:13)—on these words, Jesus brings warning to non-believers and promise to believers.

Notice how the wages will be meted out: To those who have persisted in their foolishness, rebellion, and idolatry . . . there is only the prospect of "life outside of the city" (22:15) or eternal banishment from the presence and life of God. "For the wages of sin is death" (Rom. 6:23).

Those who may go through the gates into the city and who have the right to the tree of life are those who have "washed their robes and made them white in the blood of the Lamb" (Rev. 7:14)—not those who have tried to earn "life within the city" by their own good works and self-righteousness. The dividing line in eternity is drawn between those who have merited death through their own sin, and those who are trusting in the merit of Jesus Christ won upon His cross.

There is nothing more important to understand in the book of Revelation (no, let's expand that to the whole Bible) than this: The only basis upon which we can have any confidence to stand before God on the Day of Judgment, the only hope that we can have of enjoying the glories of heaven forever is to have put our trust exclusively and completely in the finished work of Jesus Christ. Jesus has done for us what we could never do for ourselves: He has satisfied the righteous demands of God.

The apostle Paul also states these great truths:

> But now a righteousness from God, apart from law, has been made known, to which the Law and the Prophets testify. This righteousness from God comes through faith in Jesus Christ to all who believe. There is no difference, for all have sinned and fall short of the glory of God, and are justified freely by his grace through the redemption that came by Christ Jesus. God presented him as a sacrifice of atonement, through faith in his blood. He did this to demonstrate his justice, because in his forbearance he had left the sins committed beforehand unpunished—he did it to demonstrate his justice at the present time, so as to be just and the one who justifies those who have faith in Jesus. (Rom. 3:21–26)

The Bible ends with a presentation of what God has mercifully and graciously done for us in His Son, Jesus Christ. How glorious a conclusion!

As a pastor, I continue to be astounded at the number of people who occupy the pews, even in evangelical churches, who are still confused about what the "gospel" actually is. This became quite obvious as I continued to teach the study that led to this book. The freedom, joy, and hope that I witnessed emerging in the hearts of those who attended that study did not come primarily from realizing there is no hidden meaning behind every horn, eye, cough, and sneeze in the text of Revelation. The growing peace I saw coming to many Christians was not essentially the fruit of believers being freed from a lot of "Revelation baggage," unbiblical stereotypes about demons, groundless fears concerning "666," and theological arrogance about the millennium.

In all honesty, the greatest blessing I received from this study was watching Christians being set free from legalism (performance-based spirituality), mysticism (experience-centered spirituality), and antinomianism (spirituality without obedience).

Week by week we simply immersed our hearts in the "gospel of God's grace," which is so clearly communicated through the entire book of Revelation. All of us realized how easy it is to trivialize and marginalize the grace of God through the many corruptions of the gospel that abound.

The gospel itself is the main hope that is unveiled in Revelation. Jesus, the Lamb of God, has come to make atonement for the sins of God's people. He has triumphed! The writer of Hebrews says, "But when this priest had offered for all time one sacrifice for sins, he sat down at the right hand of God. Since that time he waits for his enemies to be made his footstool, because by one sacrifice he has made perfect forever those who are being made holy" (Heb. 10:12–14). Jesus made a sufficient and perfect atonement once and for all!

There is no other hope so precious and so sure. Hymnwriter Edward Mote expressed these sentiments when he penned, "My hope is built on nothing less than Jesus' blood and righteousness. No merit of my own I claim, but wholly lean on Jesus name. On Christ the solid Rock, I stand, all other ground is sinking sand." Many men and women in the Revelation Bible study ended up turning away from the "sinking sand" of self-righteousness, ritualism, cultural religion, moralism, and other forms of self-salvation. True hope is found only through abandoning ourselves to the finished work of Jesus.

The blessings for those who have "washed their robes and made them white in the blood of the Lamb" are numerous:

- The forgiveness of all sins: past, present and future.
  "All the prophets testify about him [Jesus] that everyone who believes in him receives forgiveness of sins through his name" (Acts 10:43).

Many Christians mistakenly believe that the only sins that are forgiven when someone becomes a Christian are sins committed up to the moment of conversion. However, the glory of the gospel is that God forgives *all* of our sins, including the multitude of our sins of which we are not even aware!

- Freedom from the fear of final judgment.
  "Therefore, there is now no condemnation for those who are in Christ Jesus" (Rom. 8:1).

The operative word in this great verse is "now." Christians have already been judged in Christ and now live in a permanent state of "no condemnation!"

- The imputed righteousness of Jesus Christ.
  "Now when a man works, his wages are not credited to him as a gift, but as an obligation. However, to the man who does not work but trusts God who justified the wicked, his faith is credited as righteousness. David says the same thing when he speaks of the blessedness of the man to whom God credits righteousness apart from works:

  Blessed are they
    whose transgressions are forgiven,
    whose sins are covered.
  Blessed is the man
    whose sin the Lord will never count against him"
  (Rom. 4:4–8).

So many in our Bible study were brought to great freedom when they fully realized that justification does not consist of our *being made righteous*; it is, rather, a matter of *being declared righteous* in the sight of God. Thus, we speak of our justification being by God's grace alone, which we receive through faith alone. Faith is the empty hand that receives all the good gifts of God.

- Adoption into God's family, by which we now know Him as Abba, Father.
  "For you did not receive a spirit that makes you a slave again to fear, but you received the Spirit of sonship. And by him we cry, Abba, Father. The Spirit himself testifies with our spirit that we are God's children" (Rom. 8:15–16).

There is no greater blessing than to realize that my judge has now become my loving Father. Because of the blood of Jesus, we who were once God's enemies are now His children. What wondrous love is this!

- The perpetual delight of God,
  "The LORD your God is with you,
    he is mighty to save.
  He will take great delight in you,
    he will quiet you with his love,
    he will rejoice over you with singing" (Zeph. 3:17).

The death of Jesus on the cross not only atones for (covers) the sins of God's people, it has also fully propitiated God's righteous wrath. This means that Jesus took the full force of the punishment which our sins merited. God will never be angry with us again! He is also positively delighted with us, for we are robed in the righteousness of His Son. Our heavenly Father actually rejoices over us with singing! When we studied this concept in the Revelation study we all had to repent of our unbelief! The majority of us have a hard time believing that God actually loves us as much as He says He does.

After declaring the blessedness of those who "wash their robes," Jesus reaffirms to John that it is *He* who has sent the messenger angel "to give you this testimony for the churches" (22:16). John has not written this testimony of God's glory and grace just for the benefit of the churches of the first century in Asia Minor, but also for churches in every period of history and every nation. Thank God, this includes you and me!

For the *whole* church is under the care of the One who is "the Root and the Offspring of David" (22:16). With these words Jesus reveals Himself as both King David's "root" and his "shoot." As the shoot, He is David's descendent, the promised royal Deliverer, "the Lion of the Tribe of Judah," the Messiah (Rev. 5:5; Rom. 1:3; Heb. 7:14). But as his root, He is both David's Creator and his God! He is the "bright Morning Star," (22:16) who gives His bride sufficient light until the Day when His glory will illuminate all of eternity, as the light of the sun gives way to the light of the Son (Rev. 21:23; 22:5).

An Invitation to the Thirsty

"The Spirit and the bride say, 'Come!' And let him who hears say, 'Come!' Whoever is thirsty, let him come; and whoever wishes, let him take the free gift of the water of life" (22:17).

How critical it is to see that the gospel of Jesus Christ is not just biblical or theological language to be understood, it is the good news, to be believed and received. Before the final "Amen" of the Bible, God extends the great invitation to any who would receive this "free gift of the water of life." Both the Holy Spirit and the redeemed people of God cry out to God's offer to quench the deepest thirst in the soul of man.

I close the writing of *Unveiled Hope* the way I closed our church's yearlong study of Revelation. Are you absolutely certain that you have responded to this, the greatest of all invitations? There is nothing that Mike Card and I could possibly long for more than for you who listen to the recording and read this book to make certain that the thirst of your heart has been satisfied by the "water of life."

We have considered many complex and controversial topics in this thematic study of Revelation. Perhaps you may have deep reservations about some of the interpretations offered in this book. But in the final analysis, what matters more than anything else is not what you and I think about the Great Tribulation, the Antichrist, the Rapture, the place of Israel in the history of redemption, or where we stand on a host of many other important theological issues found in the text of Revelation.

What really matters is what each of us believes about our own relationship with God. If Jesus Christ came back today, or if you were to die this hour by the sovereign appointment of God, upon what basis do you know that you would be welcomed into heaven? This is the main issue, not just in Revelation, but in the entire Bible.

Have you personally responded to this invitation to "Come"? Have you placed your complete confidence and trust in the finished work of the Lamb of God, Jesus Christ? If not, I encourage you to do so right now! *Nothing* is more important. Settling this issue may be the only reason you have been led to read this book.

After final words of warning not to tamper with the content of "this book of prophecy," Jesus again acknowledges, "Yes, I am coming soon" (22:18–20). To this great promise, the people of God of every generation respond, "Amen. Come, Lord Jesus."

The Final Word of Final Words

As we would expect, God, the quintessential author, closes His own book both masterfully and mercifully. What is our Father's final thought, His summation of the whole revelation of His Word? Consider this, the last verse in the whole Bible:

> "The grace of the Lord Jesus be with God's people"—Rev. 22:21

From the first verse of Genesis through the last verse of Revelation, the Bible is an unfolding of God's sovereign and lavish expressions of kindness and love towards His people, through the person and work of the Lord Jesus Christ. This is what the Bible means by the concept of "grace": The unilateral and unconditional favor of God expressed towards the ill-deserving.

Through God's mighty acts as Creator of all things and Redeemer of a people for Himself, we understand that this "grace" is God's Riches At Christ's Expense. God can love His people with so much passion and persistence because Jesus has fully satisfied the righteous demands of our God by His life of perfect obedience, by His substitutionary death on the cross, and by His resurrection from the dead.

Every book, every chapter, every verse in the Bible is a testimony that God is, indeed, the "God of all grace" (1 Pet. 5:10). In Revelation we have witnessed God's saving grace for all who receive forgiveness in the Lamb, His sustaining grace for His persecuted people, and His sufficient grace extended to His children called to live and to love faithfully until Jesus returns.

How, then, shall *we* respond to such a promise and benediction found in the last verse of the Revelation? May we affirm from our hearts the final "Amen" with which the Bible closes: *Yes, Lord, Your grace is sufficient for all things!*

Questions
for Reflection
and Discussion

Introduction

1. As you come to this study of the book of Revelation, what baggage are you carrying? What stereotypes, preconceived notions, apprehensions, excitement, or confusion do you bring about the last book of the Bible?

2. Based on your previous experience and current understanding, if someone were to ask you what Revelation is about, how would you respond? Who or what has had the greatest influence on how you interpret Revelation?

3. Does it bother you that Christians who are equally committed to the inspiration and authority of the Bible offer so many different perspectives on the nature, structure, intent, and meaning of the text of Revelation? How do you handle this diversity of opinion? What effect should this have on our approach to this portion of God's Word?

4. Revelation is primarily a book about hope, the unveiled hope of God's sovereign reign and saving purposes through the Lamb, Jesus Christ. How do you define hope? How does the Bible define hope? Why is the concept of hope critical for the people of God in every generation? What is your current experience of hope in this season of life? How does our contemporary culture reflect the presence or absence of hope?

Chapter One: A Vision of Jesus—The Foundation of All Hope
Revelation 1

1. What are the different images of Jesus that have settled in your heart through the years? Who or what has had the

most impact on what you believe about Jesus Christ? How has your image of Jesus affected the way you live your life?

2. How does the description of Jesus given in Revelation 1 compare with the ones that you see and hear reflected in contemporary culture and even among Christians with whom you fellowship? In contemporary Christian music, art, and worship?

3. Which of the many titles and attributes of Jesus given in Revelation 1 seize your attention? Why? In terms of your own walk with Him, what aspects of John's description of Jesus do you long to more fully experience? Why?

4. In what ways is an accurate vision of Jesus the foundation of all hope? How can false images of our Lord rob us of this hope? Martin Luther states that bad theology is the worst taskmaster of all. Do you agree?

Chapter Two: Jesus and His Bride—Hope for the Church
Revelation 2–3

1. What is your history in terms of "church life"? How would you describe your experience and involvement in a local expression of the body of Christ through the years? How would you even define the word "church"?

2. How has fresh reading of Revelation 2 and 3 affected your perspective on the importance of Christians having a deeper love for and commitment to the body of Christ? Why do you suppose so many Christians in our culture play down the importance of a serious commitment to a local church family?

3. In looking at the composite picture of the bride of Christ found in a study of the seven churches in Asia Minor, which features stand out to you as being most needed in the contemporary church? In the local church of which you are a part? Why?

4. Should God choose to bring renewal to your church family, what would it look like? What call to repentance would be given, and what changes would be made in terms of priorities and passion? What changes would be made in your own heart and life?

Chapter Three: The Hope of an Occupied Throne
Revelation 4

1. As you consider and meditate upon the "throne-room" vision that God gave John, what captures your attention and imagination? Why do you suppose that, in the midst of everything else, that which stood out to John was the occupied throne of heaven? In what ways must this have brought great encouragement to John's heart and to the hearts of those who initially received his epistle of hope?

2. What would be the benefits of securing this "throne-room" vision in your own heart? Why do we (you) desperately need to know that our God reigns? What hope is generated by such knowledge?

3. What is the difference between believing and trusting in the sovereignty of God and simply becoming a passive fatalist? What issues does the revelation of the sovereignty of God raise for us who cherish the notion of free will and autonomy?

4. God is at the center of all things in the vision given in Revelation 4. What are the implications of this for how we live our lives? What would a more God-centered worldview and lifestyle look like for those of us in the contemporary church?

Chapter Four: The Hope of the Perfected Worship of Heaven
Revelation 5:1–8; 11–14

1. Looking back through the years, how would you describe your own journey as a worshiper of God? From your earliest remembrance until now, what has been your understanding

and experience of the nature and importance of the worship of God?

2. How do you define worship? Try giving a simple definition using your own words and categories. Who and what has influenced this understanding?

3. What did you learn about the importance and nature of worship as you reflected on Revelation 4 and 5? How is the worship of heaven different from what you personally experience and what you observe in the contemporary church? What do you find yourself drawn to (and even perhaps uncomfortable with) as you take a close look at the worship of heaven?

4. Go back over the "continuums of worship" at the end of this chapter. Where would you place yourself in each of these continuums? In light of these things, how would you say the worship of your own church family could be matured and more honoring to God?

Chapter Five: The Hope of a Completed "Great Commission"
Revelation 5:9–10

1. Evangelism and Missions: two words that strike all kinds of responses in the hearts of God's people. When *you* think of these words, what comes to mind? How do you define "evangelism"? What do you understand the Great Commission to be?

2. As you read chapter 5 in *Unveiled Hope*, what issues and questions were raised? We tend to think of the Great Commission as a "job to get done." How does this chapter and, more importantly, John's vision of men and women from every race, tribe, tongue, and people around God's throne, affect your perspective on evangelism and missions? Is the Great Commission a job to accomplish or a joy to be entered into?

3. How do you suppose John's vision of a "filled-up heaven" would have impacted the hearts of the persecuted Christians of the first century? Why? How should it affect the way we view the importance of world evangelism?

4. This chapter affirms that God is far more committed to redeeming non-Christians that we are to sharing the gospel with them. Why our reluctance? What are the main reasons why you are not more personally involved in sharing God's grace with non-believers? This question is asked not to provoke you to guilt, but to love.

Chapter Six: The Hope of Purposeful Suffering
Revelation 6:1–8:1

1. Revelation 5 ends with a vision of Jesus as the One who alone is worthy to break the seals. What is the significance of this sovereign action as we consider the theme of the suffering of God's people? What hope do we receive as we realize that He is the Lord of all history, including painful history? How would this have encouraged John's readers?

2. Many of us who are baby boomers and busters came to Christ at a time when the prevailing theologies of the Christian life were rather man-centered. Strong faith and suffering were seen to be mutually exclusive. How has your own understanding of suffering been affected by this type of teaching? How has God brought you to a more Biblical balance?

3. How is your own heart comforted by the fact that you already have been eternally "sealed" by the Holy Spirit? How does the vision of the redeemed of the Lord in Revelation 7 put our present suffering into perspective? What is the relationship between suffering and world evangelism?

4. In Revelation 7:15–17 we are given a small, but glorious, glimpse of how God is going to relate to us, His children, in

heaven. What effect do you imagine this had on the persecuted Christians in Asia Minor? What effect does it have on
you? What keeps us from believing that God loves us now
the way He will love us then?

Chapter Seven: The Hope of Coming Justice
Revelation 8:2–10:11; 11:15–19

1. A major theme in the book of Revelation is the coming vindication of our God and the full manifestation of His justice
   in an unjust world. The seven trumpets announce and guarantee this day. Why do you suppose this theme would have
   been critical to the consciences of Christians in Asia Minor?
   Why is it appropriate for our own consciences to feel moral
   outrage and a deep longing for justice in the world?

2. In this chapter we learned that God is not reserving all justice and judgment for the end of the world. Even now His
   "wrath is being revealed from heaven." Where do you see
   God's judgment falling as a precursor to the final judgment?
   In light of what we can learn from the seven trumpets, what
   are the signs of His "last days judgment"?

3. Those who have been painfully victimized quite naturally
   long for justice. But when does the appropriate longing for
   justice bleed over into an unrighteous spirit of retaliation?
   What does it mean for us to relinquish the right to avenge
   ourselves to our God who alone has this right? How can we
   guard against being consumed with anger, rage, and bitterness as we look forward to the day when God will bring
   about perfect justice?

4. After reading this chapter and its corresponding section in
   the book of Revelation, how is your heart stirred to extend
   mercy to the ill-deserving? Why is it critical to always
   remember God's mercy for you, expressed in the cross, as
   you confront the many injustices that you witness both in
   the world and those brought against you personally?

Chapter Eight: The Hope of Meaningful Witness and Impact
Revelation 11:1–14

1. In this chapter of *Unveiled Hope*, the call to meaningful involvement in the culture is highlighted. Rather than retreating from the battlefront, we are to advance, even as God warns us of peril. How have you personally been affected by the "bomb shelter" mentality? In what ways have you been inclined to enter a Christian cocoon as a shield against the tide of evil?

2. Jesus calls us to be "salt and light" to the world. The apostle Peter commissions us to "live such good lives among the pagans" (1 Peter 2:12). Practically speaking, what does faithfulness to these imperatives look like? How can Christians make a difference in society?

3. Who are your models of the "two witnesses" in Revelation 11:3–14; that is, what Christians have you observed living out the grace and truth of Jesus in the marketplace? Who is taking the love of God into the public square? What can you learn from their lives and their faithful witness?

4. What is your own sphere of influence? Reflect on what it means for you to be a good steward of the days and the context into which your heavenly Father has placed you. What risk of faith is required as you purpose to be a conduit of the mercy and grace of Jesus?

Chapter Nine: The Hope of God's Perspective
Revelation 12–14

1. Perspective is one of the great gifts of God to His people. There is no area in which this gift is more needed than that of spiritual warfare. Having read this chapter in *Unveiled Hope* and chapter 12–14 of Revelation, how is your understanding of the conflict between God and Satan affected?

2. In respect to the topic of spiritual warfare, do you observe more paranoia or presumption among Christians that you know? C. S. Lewis warned that we can make two equally fatal mistakes in terms of the devil and demons: On one hand, we can be filled with obsessive fear; on the other hand, we can be dulled by a foolish naïveté.[1] Do you agree?

3. The apostle Paul stressed the importance of not being ignorant of the schemes of our enemy, Satan (2 Cor. 2:11). What can we learn about his strategies to attack God's people from this section in Revelation? How do you see the powers of darkness most at work in our culture? In our churches? In our homes?

4. How can a greater understanding of the person and work of Jesus be our most effective means of combating the works of Satan? Why does ignorance of biblical truth make Christians easy prey for the schemes of Satan?

Chapter Ten: The Hope of Victory Over Evil
Revelation 15–18

1. In this chapter we considered the importance of knowing our place in the orbit of eternity. We revolve around the Son, not vice versa. In what aspects of contemporary Christendom have you observed the tendency to relate to God as our "celestial bellhop"? Do you agree that our generation suffers from utilitarian views of God? How?

2. With the pouring forth of the seven bowls, we are introduced to the theme of the wrath of God. Certainly, the non-Christian world has a hard time with such a concept, but why do Christians have such a difficult time accepting that our God of love is also a consuming fire? What wrong notions about the wrath of God does this section of Revelation help make clear for your?

3. This chapter in *Unveiled Hope* presents the conviction that we can appreciate the concept of God's wrath and God's love only through a fresh vision of His holiness. Do you agree? Why or why not? Would you agree that this generation desperately needs a fresh vision of God's holiness? What would be the effect of such a vision?

4. How can the promise of the ultimate overthrow of evil free us and focus us as we seek to live for the glory of God? Can you think of other groups of Christians who have suffered great evil, like those of John's day, for whom these promises would have been bread from heaven? One example would be our brothers and sisters who lived during the Nazi regime.

Chapter Twelve: The Hope of the Already and the Not Yet
Revelation 20

1. Millennial Madness! I hope not. Having read this chapter in *Unveiled Hope* what are your questions about the millennium? What makes sense? What sounds like heresy? Which of the millennial positions most closely defines what you believe the book of Revelation is teaching?

2. What are the strengths of each of the three main views of the millennium? What are the weaknesses? How can we profit from discussions about topics like the millennium and events surrounding the second coming of Christ? Do you think the contemporary church emphasizes the second coming as much as it should? Explain your answer.

3. How does your own view of the millennium affect the way you live the Christian life? If you took your position more seriously how would it affect your lifestyle? Biblical theology is meant to transform us, not just inform us!

4. Why is it helpful to think in terms of the "already and the not yet"? How can this redemptive tension keep us both

faithful and expectant? To use Paul's words, do you find yourself groaning inwardly or waiting expectantly? Why are both important?

Chapter Thirteen: The Hope of the New Heavens and the New Earth
Revelation 21–22

1. Describe heaven. Go ahead . . . what do you really think heaven is going to be like? What has shaped your understanding of the eternal dwelling place of Christians? How has your understanding matured from earlier years?

2. What questions are raised by the concept of the new heavens and the new earth found in Revelation 21–22? How does this square with the standard belief of most Christians that heaven is "way out there somewhere beyond the Milky Way"? Have you ever considered the notion that heaven is actually going to be the reconstituted earth and heavens we presently enjoy?

3. What about heaven are you most looking forward to? Go back through the description in Revelation 21–22. What stands out to you? What seems almost too good to be true?

4. I take strong exception to the Christian maxim that exhorts believers not to be "so heavenly minded that they are of no earthly good." The more I study what the Bible has to say about heaven, the more I believe it is impossible to be too heavenly minded. What do you think? Could the heart filled with heaven actually be the very thing that causes us to live more expressly and sacrificially for the things that matter to the heart of God?

Epilogue: The Hope of the Gospel
Revelation 22:6–21

1. Suppose one of your friends is becoming spiritually interested and they ask you to explain the gospel. How would

you define it, and what would you highlight? Why is the content of our gospel so important?

2. What questions were raised as you read the last chapter of *Unveiled Hope*? Consider each of the "blessings" listed as benefits to those who have "washed their robes in the blood of the Lamb." Which of these stand out to you? Why? Would you agree that the gospel of God's grace seems too good to be true? Why?

3. What corruptions of the gospel do you see most pronounced in our culture? How do we tend to trivialize or marginalize the importance of God's grace in all of these false gospels? Why is a knowledge of the depth of our own thirst foundational to our experience of the riches of God's grace in the gospel?

4. Read Revelation 22:21 again and ponder its significance to you personally. As you consider your life, what expressions of the grace of the Lord Jesus are you most aware of needing? What keeps you from more fully availing yourself of "God's riches at Christ's expense"? Describe your own thirst for the grace of God. Dare to drink afresh of the "free gift of the water of life."

Notes

Introduction

1. John R. W. Stott (revised by Stephen Motyer), *Men with a Message* (Grand Rapids, MI: Wm. B. Eerdmans), 1994, p. 153.

2. Michael Wilcock, *I Saw Heaven Opened* (Downers Grove, IL: InterVarsity Press), 1975, p. 60.

3. Ibid., p. 60.

4. Ibid., p. 3.

Chapter One

1. Eugene H. Peterson, *Reversed Thunder* (New York: Harper-Collins), 1988, p. 28.

2. A. W. Tozer, *The Knowledge of the Holy* (Pennsylvania: Christian Publication), 1964, p. 11.

3. Stott, *Men with a Message*, p. 151.

4. Bruce M. Metzger, *Breaking the Code* (Nashville, TN: Abingdon Press), 1993, p. 26.

5. Thomas Howard, *Christ the Tiger* (Philadelphia: J. B. Lippincott Co.), 1967, p. 10.

6. Geffrey B. Kelley and E. Burton Nelson, eds., *A Testament of Freedom* (New York: HarperCollins), 1990, p. 484.

Chapter Two

1. George Barna, *What Americans Believe* (Ventura, CA: Regal Books), 1991, pp. 85, 294.

2. John R. W. Stott, *What Christ Thinks of the Church* (Grand Rapids, MI: Wm. B. Eerdmans), 1958, p. 72.

3. William Barclay, *The Revelation of John, Vol. 1* (Philadelphia: The Westminster Press), 1959, pp. 148-9.

4. G. B. Caird, *The Revelation of Saint John* (Peabody, MA: Hendrickson Publishers), 1966, p. 48.

5. Stott, *What Christ Thinks of the Church,* p. 116.

Chapter Four

1. Karl Barth, as quoted in J. J. vaughn-Allen, *Worship: Its Theology and Practice* (London: Lutterworth), 1965, p. 13.

2. Robert H. Mounce, *The Book of Revelation* (Grand Rapids, MI: Wm. B. Eerdmans), 1969, p. 143.

3. Stott, *What Christ Thinks of the Church,* p. 159.

4. Philip Edgcumbe Hughes, *The Book of the Revelation* (Grand Rapids, MI: Wm. B. Eerdmans), 1990, p. 82.

5. William Temple, *Readings in St. John's Gospel* (New York: MacMillan), 1939, p. 68.

6. Peterson, *Reversed Thunder.*

Chapter Six

1. Metzger, *Breaking the Code,* p. 56.

2. Hughes, *The Book of the Revelation,* p. 101.

Chapter Seven

1. Wilcock, *I Saw Heaven Opened,* pp. 94-5.

2. Ibid., pp. 97-8.

3. Chuck Coclasure, *The Overcomers* (Nashville, TN: Thomas Nelson Publishers), 1981, p. 101.

Chapter Eight

1. Hughes, *The Book of the Revelation,* p. 120.

2. Francis Schaeffer, *No Little People* (Downers Grove, IL: InterVarsity Press), 1974, p. 13.

Chapter Nine

1. Wilcock, *I Saw Heaven Opened*, p. 116.

2. Hughes, *The Book of the Revelation*, p. 136.

3. Ibid., p. 145.

4. Wilcock, p. 123-4.

5. W. Hendricksen, *More Than Conquerors* (Grand Rapids, MI: Baker Book House), 1939, p. 174-5.

6. Ibid., 179-80.

7. Hughes, p. 154-5.

8. Metzger, *Breaking the Code*, p. 77.

9. C. S. Lewis, *The Lion, the Witch and the Wardrobe*, The Chronicles of Narnia (New York: HarperCollins), 1978.

Chapter Ten

1. Metzger, *Breaking the Code*, p. 818-82.

2. Wilcock, *I Saw Heaven Opened*, p. 144.

3. Hughes, *The Book of the Revelation*, p. 180.

Chapter Eleven

1. Hughes, *The Book of the Revelation*.

Chapter Thirteen

1. Metzger, *Breaking the Code*, p. 101.

2. Hughes, *The Book of the Revelation*, p. 232.

Questions

1. C. S. Lewis, *The Screwtape Letters* (New York: Macmillan), 1982, p. 3.

SELECT BIBLIOGRAPHY

Caird, G. B. *The Revelation of Saint John*. Peabody, Mass.: Hendrickson Publishers, 1966.

Hendricksen, W. *More Than Conquerors*. Grand Rapids: Baker Book House, 1939.

Hughes, Philip Edgcumbe. *The Book of the Revelation*. Grand Rapids: William B. Eerdmans Publishing Company, 1990.

Metzger, Bruce M. *Breaking the Code*. Nashville: Abingdon Press, 1993.

Morris, Leon. *The Revelation of St. John*. Grand Rapids: William B. Eerdmans, 1969.

Mounce, Robert H. *The Book of Revelation*. Grand Rapids: William B. Eerdmans, 1977.

Palmer, Earl F. *The Communicator's Commentary, Vol. 12. 1, 2, 3 John, Revelation*. Waco, Texas: Word Books, 1982.

Peterson, Eugene H. *Reversed Thunder*. New York: Harper-Collins, 1988.

Stott, John R. W. *What Christ Thinks of the Church*. Grand Rapids: William B. Eerdmans, 1958.

Stott, John R. W. (revised by Stephen Motyer). *Men with a Message*. Grand Rapids: William B. Eerdmans, 1994.

Temple, William. *Readings in St. John's Gospel*. New York: MacMillan, 1939.

Wilcock, Michael. *I Saw Heaven Opened*. Downers Grove, Ill.: InterVarsity Press, 1975.